METAPHYSICS IN SCIENCE

Metaphysics in Science

Edited by

Alice Drewery

Blackwell
Publishing

BLACKWELL PUBLISHING
350 Main Street, Malden, MA 02148-5020, USA
9600 Garsington Road, Oxford, OX4 2DQ, UK
550 Swanston Street, Carlton, Victoria 3053, Australia

The right of Alice Drewery to be identified as the Author of the
Editorial Material in this Work has been asserted in accordance with
the UK Copyright, Designs, and Patents Act 1988.

First published 2006 by Blackwell Publishing Ltd

First published in RATIO, an international journal of analytic
philosophy, volume 18, No. 4.

Library of Congress Cataloging-in-Publication Data has been applied for

ISBN 978-1-4051-4514-5

A catalogue record for this title is available from the British Library.

Set in 11 on 12 pt New Baskerville
by SNP Best-set Typesetter Ltd., Hong Kong

For further information on
Blackwell Publishing, visit our website:
www.blackwellpublishing.com

CONTENTS

INTRODUCTION

Alice Drewery

1. Metaphysics and science

There is a complex relationship between metaphysics and science. They seem to aim towards the same goal, that of explaining the fundamental nature of the world. One way we might characterise the difference between them is in terms of method: science proceeds empirically or a posteriori, whereas metaphysics proceeds a priori. This might explain some of the criticisms of scholastic metaphysics which was accused of constraining science by focussing too much on the a priori. Conversely, with the development of the new scientific method in the seventeenth and eighteenth centuries, western philosophy became dominated by similar empirical methods which threatened to trivialise metaphysics, a trend which is still visible in some places today. However, to suggest that this difference in method marks the boundary between science and metaphysics is far too simple. As some of the papers in this volume illustrate, the correct method of metaphysics, and the extent to which its conclusions are empirically based, is a matter of controversy. And it is naïve to suggest that science proceeds without a priori assumptions which underlie the whole project of scientific enquiry. The current revival in metaphysics treads a middle ground, between the extreme empiricism which rejects metaphysics entirely, and extreme rationalism, which threatens to make metaphysics a mere exercise in system-building with no relevance to the world around us.

In the twentieth century, this extreme empiricism and naturalism led to a rejection of metaphysics as fundamentally unscientific, and a deep suspicion of many of the basic questions with which metaphysics traditionally deals. What exists is what science tells us exists. Sentences are only meaningful if empirical verification is possible, hence the extent to which modal discourse is meaningful is highly attenuated, at best. Philosophical discussion of subjects such as causation, laws of nature and the status of categories or kinds was for the most part reduced to minimal claims about what is observable or what is expedient for science. A change occurred with the development of modal logic in the 1960s, and with the apparent possibility of a coherent semantics for modal discourse. This paved the way for future work in many areas where modality plays a central role – laws, dispositions, counterfactuals, causation, even essentialism. The last was dramatically pushed to centre stage with the work of Kripke and Putnam in the 1970s and with the sudden recognition of an apparently new style of argument for the possibility of substantive a priori knowledge and for some necessary truths to be within the compass of science.

The corresponding development of metaphysics since that time has been great, but perhaps the area where it is still most resisted is that of philosophy of science. While much has been written on certain metaphysical topics that are relevant to science, particularly causation, laws, and counterfactuals, there is still a resistance to metaphysics within some areas of the philosophy of science, no doubt due to the worries about methodology stemming from an empiricist and naturalist perspective. Nonetheless, those working in these areas of metaphysics and others, including scientific realism, dispositions, and the nature of natural kinds, are beginning to develop a critical mass, and so the field of 'metaphysics in science' is a popular and growing one. This collection adds to an increasing literature, and offers a selection of perspectives on various topics in this important area.

2. Themes in scientific metaphysics

Realism and methodology

Like most philosophers who take science seriously, metaphysicians of science are for the most part scientific realists. However, there are large differences between different scientific metaphysicians in respect of *how much* they think science can tell us. The main question arising here is what, if anything, science can tell us about metaphysics itself.

This question recurs throughout all the papers in the volume, more or less directly. It is the main focus in the exchange between Ellis and Psillos, who disagree as to whether scientific realism commits one to a particular kind of physicalist, non-Humean ontology. It is also a major concern of Heil, who argues that Ellis's six-category ontology is unnecessary, and that a Lockean two-category ontology will do all the same work. In Mumford's paper, the concern arises in the guise of whether essentialism itself can be justified purely empirically, or requires independent argument. And in Bird's paper, scientific concerns are used to defend a dispositionalist view of properties. Ellis engages with all these arguments in his final reply.

These sorts of concerns, of course, are not new. The proper methodology of metaphysics is a perennial question, and indeed one striking feature of Ellis's work has been the challenge to the empiricist equation of possibility with conceivability. (Although in the context of Ellis's work this equation is most associated with Hume, it is originally and most clearly found in Descartes, and early criticisms can be found in the work of contemporary commentators.) The acceptance of the idea that we can separate epistemic and metaphysical possibility is an obvious development from the new ways of thinking about modality following the rehabilitation of modal logic in the 1960s. However, it is not so clear that a replacement for the standard thought-experiment-based methodology of metaphysics is going to be easy to find. This is especially so since the status of metaphysical possibility is exactly an object of debate, and so it may be that the divide between essentialists such as Ellis and neo-Humeans becomes partly a debate about methodology, thus complicating the issues further. For example, in the exchange between Ellis and Psillos in this volume, both Ellis and Psillos agree that science commits us to the existence of causal powers. But Psillos denies this must lead to a non-Humean ontology, as Ellis claims, for science does not distinguish between the Humean and intrinsicalist account of causal powers. Strictly speaking, this is probably true: there is by hypothesis no empirical difference in the observable phenomena, only in the metaphysics. But it might be argued that science tells us that it is *not possible* for an object which has up till now possessed a certain causal power to behave in a different way, as the Humean account entails. The Humean may object that the only way to ground this claim of possibility is to assume the very point in question, that it is essential to some object that it has certain causal powers. Hence the debate may deteriorate into a flat clash of intuitions.

Perhaps partly for these reasons, another kind of argument in favour of his view is offered by Ellis, that of the argument-by-display (see Ellis 2001: 262, discussed by Mumford in this volume). This is often associated with the work of David Lewis

on modal realism, the idea being that in the absence of compelling independent reasons for or against it, we assess a metaphysical framework based on its costs and benefits. The problem
with such an approach is that the evaluation of costs and benefits
can itself be highly controversial, and this is seen in Mumford's
assessment of Ellis's metaphysics. It seems, then, that the issue of
methodology is one which is still evolving in the context of the
current debate.

The dispositional and the categorical

Another feature of several of the papers in this volume is their
focus on the nature of dispositions. The non-Humean approach
to dispositions is characterised in several ways. There is Ellis's
claim that he is rejecting a Humean 'passivist' view of the world
in favour of an active world of causal powers, or (in terms of the
ontological categories accepted by various protagonists, particularly Ellis) dynamic universals, instantiated by particular causal
processes. Alternatively, Shoemaker's (1980) view of properties as
collections (or 'bestowers') of causal powers is used to argue for
a view of properties as essentially dispositional or dynamic. As
already observed, Ellis argues for the reality of intrinsic causal
powers, claiming this is a commitment of scientific theories, a
claim Psillos rejects. Heil and Bird discuss the question of whether
all properties can be essentially dispositional, and if so, how categorical properties can be understood. Ellis, in his final reply,
responds to these discussions with a new suggestion about the
relationship between the dispositional and the categorical.

We should take some care with the terms in which this debate
is couched. As already observed above, the mere acceptance of
causal powers or dispositions, even those prefaced with the term
'real' (as in *real* causal powers), is something which all but the
most extreme eliminativists will accept. The difference between
Ellis's position and a standard Humean view is in whether any of
these dispositions are either *irreducible* or *intrinsic* to the objects
which possess them. As already noted, Psillos argues that
Humeans can happily believe in causal powers and in dispositional properties, though these are ascribed on the basis of regularities in which the objects in question participate and are
therefore not irreducible. Beebee (2004: 336–7) even challenges
Ellis's charge of passivism against the Humean, claiming that the
idea of a passive world, pushed and pulled about by the laws of

nature, is profoundly un-Humean. The difference between Ellis and the Humean can less controversially be put in terms of onto-logical priority or dependence. For the Humean, the dispositions of objects are dependent upon their categorical properties and the laws (regularities) in which those objects participate. So dis-positions or causal powers are neither intrinsic nor irreducible. For Ellis and others of his persuasion (e.g., Molnar 2003) there can be irreducible causal powers, and causal powers which are intrinsic to their bearers.

Natural kinds and essentialism

The natural kind structure of the world, described and motivated in Ellis (2001, 2002), is another consequence of taking scientific theories at face value, according to Ellis. The metaphysical status of kinds is challenged by Heil and Mumford, who argue that the same work can be done without some of the metaphysical com-mitments of Ellis's theory. One such commitment is essentialism, and in particular the essentialism of Kripke and Putnam. I have already noted the effect of their work on the semantics of natural kind terms in the 1970s, and while there have been challenges to their arguments, their conclusions are widely accepted. Ellis's arguments for essentialism are distinct from Kripke's and Putnam's, though, and he focuses on the practice of science and classification, arguing that this practice requires a hierarchy of objectively distinct kinds defined by their essential properties.

Ellis, then, is concerned with the essences of kinds and prop-erties, rather than the essences of individuals. Moreover, his is supposed to be a substantive theory of essence, distinguished from a merely identificatory theory, which would just give the properties that are necessary and sufficient for membership of a kind. But one question is how such a theory is to be worked out. Clearly, Ellis wishes to distance himself from the thin, modalist conception of essence, where the essence of a kind would be given by the set of properties it is necessary that every member of a kind possesses. Perhaps he might instead endorse a more substantive notion based on real definition, as defended by Fine (1994); this is suggested by his remark that 'the essential properties of a kind include all of the intrinsic properties and structures that together *make a thing the kind of thing it is*' (2001: 55, my italics). Mumford's criticism of Ellis's essentialism is that a cost-benefit analysis does not show the theory in a good light, for there is no added value over and above the assumptions which the theory makes. We might put this in another way (cf. Drewery 2005): one supposed virtue of Ellis's theory is that the laws of nature are grounded in worldly necessary connections. But these worldly necessary connections just *are* the connections between a kind and its essential properties. So in assuming that there are essences of kinds, one gets laws of nature for free. But there is no ontological dependence or grounding here; law statements are just partial statements of the essences of kinds, and the essence of a kind simply is the set of laws in which it participates.

In his reply to Mumford, Ellis argues that what distinguishes an essential from an accidental property of a kind is that the former but not the latter possesses an explanatory power; like Lockean real essences, they *explain* the observable properties of an object. This explanatory power derives from the fact that the essential properties are those which are *intrinsic* to a kind member, where intrinsicality is given a causal definition. Whether a full account of essence can be worked out based on this conception of intrinsicality remains to be seen, but it suggests that there will be a close connection between essences, laws and kinds, and we should not therefore expect a reductive account of any one of these in terms of the others. (For detailed discussion of how Aristotle's essentialism requires the interdependence of definition and explanation, see Charles (2000), especially chapter 10.)

3. This volume

I now turn to a brief introduction of the papers in this volume, and the points to which Ellis responds in his reply which forms the final paper.

Brian Ellis's paper 'Physical Realism' summarises much of his position on the new essentialism (as he calls it in *The Philosophy of Nature*). As already outlined, Ellis argues that physical realism, his version of scientific realism, commits us both to the existence of irreducibly modal facts and to physicalism. So a physical realist cannot also be a Humean. This is because the only way to account for the diverse truth-makers of scientific propositions is to embrace a modal ontology: specifically, one containing a hierarchy of substantial natural kinds and of kinds of event or process, where these kinds are individuated in terms of intrinsic physical properties of the relevant objects or events which they categorise. The commitment to physicalism arises from the rejection of abstract objects (e.g., numbers, possible worlds, and idealisations such as points, perfect gases, etc.) because 'there is no plausible ontology that would accommodate them' (p. 7). Although this may seem rather quick, Ellis's aim here is to contrast those scientific propositions which we can take at face value and those we cannot, the latter being descriptions of idealisations, models or other theoretical constructs which, while they may well be useful to science, do not describe reality. The traditional argument for scientific realism has overlooked something important in not making this distinction, which should, Ellis claims, be reflected in ontology.

In 'Scientific Realism and Metaphysics', Stathis Psillos criticises these two commitments to physicalism and non-Humeanism. On the former, he challenges Ellis's claim that a commitment to realism alone can rule out certain kinds of entity from one's ontology. Realists, he argues, must at least in the first instance take scientific propositions at face value, and then enter into the debate as to whether the entities to which they appear to be committed are sui generis or not. Realism itself does not legislate between pluralism, reductionism and eliminativism about certain classes of facts: this is a further debate. To say, as Ellis does, that certain scientific propositions do not describe reality, is to presuppose an eliminativist line about their truth-makers. But this cannot be part of a realist approach to science, since realists must start by taking scientific propositions at face value. Similarly, Psillos argues that scientific realism does not by itself establish the existence of necessary connections in nature. This is again because science cannot tell us whether causal powers are sui generis or reducible. All science tells us is that there are causal powers – not whether these are ineliminable or intrinsic.

John Heil is also concerned with the ontology to which science commits us. Ellis argues for a six-category ontology, containing substantive universals, which are instantiated by particular substances (objects), dynamic universals, which are instantiated by particular events, and (property) universals, which are instantiated by their tropes. Heil describes what he calls a Locke-world, which contains only concrete particulars: objects and modes (tropes). On such an ontology, we can still admit essences and kinds, and, Heil argues, can still do science in just the same way as Ellis envisages, and without some of the problems that arise when we try to characterise the relationships between universals. Heil also raises the question of where categorical properties fit into the picture (see also Bird's paper). Are there fundamental and non-relational categorical properties? If not, how are the paradigm non-fundamental categorical properties such as shape, size and number supposed to emerge from merely dispositional properties at the fundamental level, a problem sometimes referred to as 'Swinburne's regress' (Ellis 2002: 171–6)? Heil favours a Lockean solution according to which properties are both qualities and powers. Primary qualities are powerful qualities: '[o]bjects' shapes, sizes, and densities determine how they behave or would behave' (p. 44). Ellis responds to both these criticisms at the end of the volume, reiterating the case for the six-category ontology to explain the hierarchical structure of reality, and offering a new perspective on the relationship between the dispositional and the categorical in response to Heil's and Bird's criticisms.

Stephen Mumford challenges Ellis's essentialism, arguing that we can accept the hierarchy of natural kinds without embracing essentialism and the corresponding necessities which it generates. Mumford accepts that objects may have intrinsic causal powers, and that there are natural kinds, though by Ellis's *objectivity* and *categorical distinctness* criteria (2001: 19; see also Mumford 2004: 110, where this is called the 'no continuum argument'), their existence is a contingent matter. He asks, though, why we should accept that some characterising properties of a kind are essential to that kind. He agrees with Salmon (1982), who argues that the Kripke-Putnam arguments about a posteriori necessities rely on additional premises about the natures of kinds which cannot be justified by science alone. These additional premises can be and have been challenged by anti-essentialists. Ellis's reason for adopting essentialism is an argument by display, or a species of cost-benefit analysis (see also above). But Mumford argues that in order to acquire these benefits, one must assume the very results the theory is supposed to deliver. Mumford finally offers an alternative account of natural kinds, which does not rely on essentialism. Kinds are natural types of objects-bearing-modes, which are 'constituted by the omintemporal totality of their member objects' (p. 60).

Alexander Bird's paper defends an extension of Ellis's view, on which the fundamental properties, i.e., those which appear in the fundamental laws of nature, are all essentially dispositional properties. The result is that the mere existence of such a property entails that (at least some) laws involving it are metaphysically necessary; adding the requirement that what holds for one law holds for all laws yields the claim that all laws are necessary. Bird then argues that the dispositionalist account of properties is preferable to a categoricalist approach, since the latter entails quidditism: the position that fundamental properties have no essential powers. But quidditism entails that we are necessarily ignorant of the natures of fundamental properties, and further that properties are entirely separable from the way objects which bear them behave. Adopting dispositionalism thus concurs with our intuitions about the identity of properties, just as Shoemaker (1980) claimed. Finally, Bird addresses the worry that some fundamental properties might not be essentially dispositional. He suggests that, ultimately, discoveries in physics might suggest that all fundamental properties can be seen as dispositional.

References

Beebee, H. (2004). Review of B. Ellis, *Scientific Essentialism* and *The Philosophy of Nature*, *Mind* 113: 334–40.

Charles, D. (2000). *Aristotle on Meaning and Essence*. Oxford: Oxford University Press.

Drewery, A. (2005). 'Essentialism and the Necessity of the Laws of Nature', *Synthese* 144: 381–96.

Ellis, B. (2001). *Scientific Essentialism*. Cambridge: Cambridge University Press.

—— (2002). *The Philosophy of Nature*. Chesham: Acumen.

Fine, K. (1994). 'Essence and Modality', *Philosophical Perspectives* 8: 1–16.

Molnar, G. (2003). *Powers*, ed. S. Mumford. Oxford: Oxford University Press.

Mumford, S. (2004). *Laws in Nature*. London: Routledge.

Salmon, N. (1982). *Reference and Essence*. Oxford: Blackwell.

Shoemaker, S. (1980). 'Causality and Properties', in *Time and Cause*, ed. P. van Inwagen. Dordrecht: Reidel Publishing Co.: 109–35.

CHAPTER 1

PHYSICAL REALISM

Brian Ellis

1. Scientific realism

I suppose scientific realism to be a thesis about the nature of reality. It is, therefore, primarily a metaphysical thesis. Nevertheless, there is a philosophical programme known as 'scientific realism', which is as much about the nature and role of scientific theory, and the epistemic status and semantic implications of its laws and theories, as it is about metaphysics. This paper is critical of the programme, but not primarily of the thesis. I call my own version of the thesis 'physical realism', because the metaphysical thesis that I wish to defend is a sophisticated physicalist one that is inspired more by 1960s physicalism and the new essentialism, than by the programme of scientific realism.

The programme is admirably presented and discussed in Stathis Psillos's (1999) book on the subject. This book presents an overall perspective on scientific realism that is comprehensive, fair and lucid. Its major defect is one that it shares with most other justifications of scientific realism, viz. that it presents the case for realism as a two-stage argument from the empirical success of science, to the truth, or approximate truth, of its dominant theories, to the reality of the things and processes that these theories appear to describe. Formally this argument would be sound, if one had an adequate theory of truth to carry the metaphysical burden. But no such theory of truth is developed in Psillos's book (or anywhere else, to my knowledge), and one is left to speculate on what ontology might be implied by the truth of science's well-established theories.

Rather than try to develop such a theory of truth here, I shall tackle the metaphysical task directly – my aim being to give an account of the nature of reality that will adequately explain why science has been able to construct the scientific image that it has. In presenting my argument, I shall presuppose no concept of truth other than that of epistemic rightness (as developed in Ellis 1990). For it is useful to separate the epistemic issues from the metaphysical ones. To address the epistemic issue of whether a proposition is true or not, we have only to consider whether the grounds for claiming it to be true are sufficient to justify the claim. If the proposition is an empirical one, then we might consider the empirical evidence that is available to decide whether or not it puts the issue beyond doubt. If it is a proposition of mathematics, then we might consider its proof, or, if that is beyond us, the merits of the claim that it has been conclusively proven. The epistemic concept of truth is thus straightforwardly applicable to propositions of all sorts, whatever their field, and we do not need a metaphysical theory of what would make a proposition of a given kind true or false in order to use it. For truth, in the minimalist sense of epistemic rightness, is metaphysically neutral.

I take it that the following propositions are all true in the minimalist epistemic sense:

(a) Sugar is soluble in water
(b) It is impossible to produce a perpetual motion machine of the second kind
(c) To a first approximation, every body attracts every other body in the universe with a force that is inversely proportional to the square of the distance between them
(d) The speed of light is the same with respect to all inertial systems
(e) $e^{i\theta} = cos\theta + isin\theta$
(f) There are just five regular polyhedra
(g) The efficiency of a Carnot engine working between the Absolute temperatures T_2 and T_1 is $(T_2 - T_1)/T_2$
(h) Ideal markets ensure Pareto-optimality
(i) Paracetamol relieves pain
(j) The subject is thinking about a horse

But none of these statements is metaphysically transparent. For it is not clear what ontology is required to accommodate them. Are there any real causal powers, necessities, forces, or inertial systems in the world? What do mathematical theorems describe? What are the truthmakers of ideal theories? To what categories do mental events and states belong?

I shall not try to answer all of these questions here. My more modest aim is to argue that scientific realists need to be able to answer such questions, if their position is to be tenable. It is not enough for them to argue that the established laws and theories of science are mostly true, or at least approximately true, as though this were the end of the matter. In my view, this is just the beginning. The real work has yet to be done in spelling out the metaphysical implications of this conclusion.

Psillos's account, like that of so many others, leaves the real work to others. For the common assumption seems to be that the principal worry for scientific realists is the question of whether established scientific theories are true. Certainly, the main challenge to scientific realism has come from this direction. But, even if the question of the truth of established theories could be settled decisively in favour of scientific realism, the ontological question would remain. For the correspondence theory of truth on which realists usually rely is far too weak and indecisive to carry the metaphysical burden of the argument for scientific realism. In putting forward his semantic thesis, Psillos advises us to take scientific theories 'at face value', and see them as 'truth-conditioned descriptions of their intended domains, both observable and unobservable'. But how, I ask, is one supposed to do this? I have no trouble in taking 'The cat is on the mat' as a truth-conditioned assertion about the domestic scene at home. Nor am I puzzled about how to understand the statement 'Oxygen has atomic number eight.' The ontological implications of these claims seem clear enough. But many, if not most, scientific claims are metaphysically much more obscure than these, and one cannot just read their ontological commitments off the page.

Originally, a scientific realist was simply one who believed the world to be more or less as the scientific image implies it is. Scientific realists, such as Smart (1963) and Sellars (1963), believed it to be a mind-independent reality, whose content and structure is gradually, if imperfectly, being revealed to us by the methods of empirical science. No scientific realist at any time has believed that the world is exactly as current science depicts, because they would all concede that some of our currently accepted theories are bound to be superseded, and lead to significant changes in our beliefs about the world. Nevertheless, scientific realists have generally been persuaded that such changes are now unlikely to lead to the wholesale rejection of the current scientific image. Some big changes may occur, they concede, but they think that radical changes, such as those that have historically occurred in astronomy, dynamics, chemistry, heat theory, geology, and biology, are unlikely to recur in any of these well-established areas. And no scientific realist believes that the very existence of a mind-independent reality is ever likely to be seriously challenged by scientific advances.

But even if this optimism should prove to be ill founded, and profound scientific revolutions were later to occur in most fields, belief in the ontology that seems to be required for current science might still be the most rational metaphysical position. For such a metaphysic would at least be the best explanation that is currently available of the empirical successes and failures of science, even if it were to prove to be inadequate for ultimate science.

Most scientific realists of the 1960s would probably have called themselves 'physicalists'. For the physicalists of this period (e.g., Smart 1963; Sellars 1963) were those who believed the world to be essentially a physical world that is more or less as the physicists of that era believed it to be – and nothing more besides. Thus, they accepted realism about the scientific image, and combined it with physical reductionism. Consequently, the early physicalists rejected the view that there are any essentially mental events or processes, i.e. events or processes occurring in people's minds, that could not, even in principle, be reduced to physical ones. The world, they argued, is really just a physical world, and all mental events are really just physical events. This position seems to me to be basically correct – but only as far as it goes. The physicalism of the 1960s needs to be supplemented in various ways to account for causal laws, natural necessities (and impossibilities), and truths about natural kinds, properties, and relationships. For without a much richer ontology than Smart or Sellars ever envisaged, many of the various kinds of truths encountered in the sciences would lack truthmakers. A richer ontology of the kind required was argued for in Ellis (1987), and developed in *Scientific Essentialism* (Ellis 2001).

2. The new scientific image

The new scientific image of the world is an elaboration and development of the old one. Like the old one, the new scientific image is of a basically *physical world*. It is a world in which all objects are really physical objects, all events and processes are physical, and in which physical objects can have only physical properties (Ellis 1976). To elaborate this position, I now propose the following definitions:

1. A *physical object* is anything that has energy, or consists of things that have energy.
2. A *physical event* is any change of energy distribution in the universe.
3. A *physical process* is any causally or inertially connected sequence of physical events
4. A *physical property* is any real property, possession of which would make a difference to at least one kind of physical process involving that object.

I think that most physicalists of the 1960s would have accepted this picture, or something very like it.

The new scientific image differs from the old one in a number of important respects. Firstly, it embraces the idea that the world is a highly structured reality (Ellis 2001, 2002), in which there are objective hierarchies of distinct kinds of things in each of the two principal categories of existence.

1. There is an objective hierarchy of distinct kinds of objects or substances generated by the species relation. This hierarchy is nowhere more evident than in the field of chemistry. For there are known to be literally tens, if not hundreds, of thousands of categorically distinct kinds of chemical substances, with laws at all levels of generality relating to them.
2. There is an objective hierarchy of distinct kinds of events or processes. For example, there is a hierarchy of kinds of causal processes that is formally like the hierarchy of kinds of substances, since every different chemical equation describes a distinct kind of process, and the kinds of processes that may be described are evidently related as species in a hierarchy.

Secondly, the instances of the kinds in these two hierarchies all have intrinsic physical properties in virtue of which they are things of the kinds they are. Consequently, the new scientific image of the world implies that reality has a definite modal structure (Ellis 2001, 2002). For the natural properties that exist in the world must be supposed to include a range of causal powers, and, realism about these causal powers should be as much part of the new scientific image of the world as realism about the physical objects or events that possess them. Consequently, the new scientific image of reality is not that of a Humean world of logically independent events, as Smart's image of reality undoubtedly was, but rather that of a world of objects of categorically distinct kinds necessarily involved in the natural events and processes that are the appropriate displays of their genuine causal powers in the contingent circumstances of their existence.

3. Do the laws and theories of science truly describe reality?

According to the proposed definitions of the physical, the category of physical objects includes all of the fundamental particles and fields of the kinds that are recognised in physics, all of the atoms and molecules that chemists talk about, all of the cells and organisms of biology; in short, just about all of the things that most scientific realists think they should believe in. However, the category of physical objects does not include any of the Platonic objects of mathematics, logic, or modal semantics. Nor does it include the idealised objects of abstract model theories. It does not, for example, include geometrical points, perfect gases, perfectly reversible heat engines, inertial systems, or ideal incompressible fluids in steady flow in uniform gravitational fields, even though there are laws of physics that seemingly tell us about such things. Nor does the category of physical objects include Newtonian extrinsic forces, although there are laws of action, combination and distribution of such forces. In my view, these things are not real, and the propositions that are supposed to be true of them need not be even approximately true of real things. Therefore, a scientific realist should not, in my view, be required to believe in them.

Yet the argument from the success of science, to the approximate truth of its dominant theories, to the reality of the theoretical entities seemingly referred to in these theories, would appear to lead to a different conclusion. For it seems to require belief in the Platonic entities of mathematics, the theoretical entities of abstract model theories, and the forces of Newtonian physics. There are, of course, many scientific realists who do believe in some or all of these things. But a physical realist has no good cause to do so.

There is probably no more successful or well-established branch of scientific knowledge than arithmetic, which I take to be the theory of numerical relationships. But scientific realists are surely not required to believe in the reality of any abstract particulars, such as numbers. There are, it is true, some scientific realists, who do believe in numbers, e.g. those who rely what I call 'the strong argument for scientific realism' (see my 1992 critical notice of Bigelow and Pargetter's *Science and Necessity*) to argue from the predictive success of number theory to the conclusion that numbers exist. Nevertheless, I do not think that we should accept them. For there is no plausible ontology that would accommodate them. Similarly, there is the case of geometry. The theories of spatial and spatiotemporal relationships are certainly of fundamental importance in physics. And such relationships undoubtedly exist. But the primary theoretical entities of the geometry, viz. geometrical points, are neither physical objects, nor universals, nor members of any other plausible ontological category. Therefore, we should not have to believe in them.

Geometrical points in space are not to be confused with the mass-points of Newtonian gravitational theory, which are abstract entities of a different kind. For Newtonian mass-points are supposed to be located in space, rather than be elements of it. As such, they are supposed to be capable of moving about in space, and consequently of occupying different geometrical points at different times. But mass-points are not physical objects either. Nor are they members of any other acceptable ontological category. Rather, they are just the idealised objects of an abstract model theory. It is true that mass-points are supposed to have mass, and therefore energy. But mass-points cannot be accepted as physical entities any more than geometrical points can be. For mass-points exist only as abstract representations of physical objects, idealised as having point-like locations, and postulated as having masses so that they can, theoretically at least, interact with each other. Of course, a theory that employs such abstract entities is not a realistic one. Presumably, it was never intended to be. Nevertheless, physicists, who wish to understand how clouds of real particles behave, might do very well to consider how clouds of point-masses would behave. This is just the sort of thing that any abstract model theory does. It does not, and is not intended to, describe the world, but to model it, and so reveal its underlying structure. One would have to be very naïve to suppose that Newton, or anyone else, ever believed in the point-masses they postulated in their theories.

Consider also Sadi Carnot's theory of the heat engine (1824). After 180 years, Carnot's theory is still the fundamental one in the area, and every student of thermodynamics has to have a good understanding of it. But Carnot's model of the heat engine is consciously not realistic. Carnot sought to explain the workings of the heat engine by abstracting from the heat losses, and other causes of inefficiency, that occur in all real heat engines, in order that he might consider the fundamental nature of the processes involved in producing useful work. Carnot was a caloricist, and his hypothesis was that heat produces useful work in the process of falling from a higher to a lower temperature level, just as water in a water mill does in falling from a higher reservoir to a lower one. We now know that Carnot was wrong about this, and, according to Psillos, there is evidence that Carnot himself had doubts about the nature of the process (although you would never know this from Carnot's original paper). Whether this was so or not, Carnot was not wrong about the essentials. Essentially, work is produced by maintaining a gas at a high temperature while allowing it to expand isothermally, allowing it to expand further adiabatically, so that its temperature drops, compressing it isothermally at this lower temperature, and then compressing it further adiabatically to restore it to its original pressurised state at the higher temperature. The work done in a given cycle is the excess of the work done by the gas in the expansion phase over the work required in the compression phase.

Carnot's model of the heat engine was an idealisation of this process. The temperature of the source of heat required for the isothermal expansion was assumed to be the same as that of the expanding gas, so that no temperature differences would appear, and hence no heat losses would occur, during this phase. Likewise, the temperature of the heat sink was assumed to be the same as that of the working substance throughout the isothermal compression phase. The adiabatic expansion and compression phases of the cycle were supposed to occur in a perfectly insulated cylinder, so that no heat losses would occur during these phases either. The whole process was supposed to involve a perfectly lubricated cylinder to eliminate the possibility of work losses due to friction. Obviously, no real heat engine even approximates to this ideal, and the efficiencies of real heat engines are orders of magnitude less efficient than Carnot's theory implies they could be. But Carnot's theory is nevertheless the fundamental one in the theory of heat engines. For, using Carnot's model, and what is now known as the Second Law of Thermodynamics, it is not hard to demonstrate that:

a) The efficiency of a Carnot engine is independent of the nature of the working substance, and is a function only of the temperature limits through which it operates. Specifically, $e = (T_2 - T_1)/T_2$, where T_2 is the Absolute temperature of the source, and T_1 that of the sink,

b) The Carnot engine is the most efficient possible for any heat engine operating between these temperature limits.

But neither Carnot, nor anyone else at the time, ever thought that Carnot's engine was anything other than a theoretical fiction. So, Psillos's semantic thesis, which would require us to take such well-established theories such as Carnot's 'at face value', and see them as 'truth-conditioned descriptions of their intended domains', does not seem to be good advice. Good theories in established fields in the mature sciences, even seminal ones, need not be realistic.

The case of forces, conceived of in the manner of Newton as extrinsic to the bodies on which they operate, is different again. According to my proposed definition of physicality, Newtonian forces are not physical objects, since they do not have energy. The action of a Newtonian force is a physical event, since it necessarily involves some change in the object on which it acts. But strangely, the production of such a force is not. The object that produces the force is not affected by the fact of its production; it is affected only by the reaction that its action produces. So, if Newtonian forces are objects, then they are very curious objects. As Robert Mayer once noted: 'If gravity be called a force, a cause is supposed which produces effects without itself diminishing, and incorrect conceptions of the causal connexion of things are thereby fostered' (Magie 1935: 199). Theoretically, Newtonian forces are always eliminable from physics. We need only combine the laws of their production with those of their combination and action to obtain laws of distribution of their effects. But, in practice, we cannot always do this, because the resultant forces are often the products of too many and too complex factors, and the measurements and calculations that would be required to eliminate the forces would be beyond us, even if there were some point in trying to do it. So, should we be realists about forces of the kind that Newton described? The standard arguments for scientific realism clearly say 'yes'. They are, after all, theoretical entities in causal roles in highly successful theories in one of the maturest of all of the sciences. But a physical realist should say 'no'. Forces are not physical entities. Therefore, however useful they may be as theoretical entities, they must be rejected in ontology.

There are, therefore, some very good reasons for thinking that established physical theory is not ontologically transparent. Firstly, the ontological implications of established propositions about Platonic entities, such as numbers, geometrical points, Euclidean planes, propositions and possible worlds, simply cannot be read off from the page, as though they were unproblematic. There are, of course, realists about all of these things. But according to physical realism, if one wishes to be a realist about any of them, then one must construe them as universals of some kind. For these are the only kinds of physical entities in a physical realist's ontology that they could possibly be. But mathematical entities do not appear to be universals either.[1] Secondly, the ontological implications of laws about theoretical ideals are not obvious. Certainly, there are well-known and well-established laws that purport to be about ideal things of one kind or another. For example, there are established laws of ideal gases, inertial systems, black body radiators, ideally free markets, perfect competition, and so on. And since these laws are all presumably true in the minimalist epistemic sense, a scientific realist who accepts Psillos's semantic thesis would appear to be committed to the reality of all of them. But according to physical realism these entities do not exist as physical objects. They are, rather, the objects of ideal theories, which are not intended to describe the world, as Psillos's semantic thesis requires. Thirdly, there are objects of conceptual convenience, such as forces. There is good reason to think that forces are not physical entities. Certainly, they are not physical objects, events or properties, as I have defined them. Therefore, there is good reason not to include them in a scientific ontology. Therefore, scientific realists should not, qua scientific realists, be committed to their existence. Psillos's semantic thesis should therefore be rejected.

4. Explaining science metaphysically

The best argument for physical realism is not an argument from the empirical success of science to the truth of it laws and theo-

---

[1]   My positive account includes a range of numerical and spatio-temporal relationships as genuine universals, but does not embrace numbers or geometrical points. See Ellis (1987).

ries to the reality of its theoretical entities. For no such argument is able to be as metaphysically discriminating as it should be about the different kinds of theories in science, or the different kinds of theoretical entities that are postulated. The best argument is the one that derives from the extraordinary nature of the new scientific image or the world, and the attempt to explain it metaphysically. For the question that needs to be addressed is this: How is the sophisticated, relatively stable, scientific image of the world that is the result of the last two or three centuries of scientific work to be explained? Don't look at it theory by theory, I say, and seek to justify the ontologies of the most successful ones in terms of what these theories are able to predict. Look at the picture as a whole. This is what no hypothesis other than a global metaphysical theory such as physical realism can possibly explain. The image that the most successful scientific theories have systematically constructed for us is an extraordinary one. It is an image of a world that consists entirely of things belonging to an elaborate, strongly interconnected, hierarchical structure of categorically distinct kinds (of chemical substances, particles, fields, etc.), and involved in natural processes which themselves are organised in a natural hierarchy of categorically distinct kinds. Moreover, the ways in which they are involved are seen as depending on their specific causal powers, capacities and propensities, and the spatiotemporal relations between them. It is a picture, not of a mechanistic world, but of a world that is every bit as tightly organised and structured as Paley's watch.

According to the Maxwell-Bridgman theory of physical reality, a real thing always manifests itself in more than one way. A basketball not only looks round; it feels round, and it rolls. A basketball that manifested itself only visually, or only from one point of view, might well be dismissed as a chimera. But one that you can catch and throw into a basket is not a chimera – it is the real thing. Much the same is true of the theoretical entities of science that most of us believe in. The same entities crop up again and again in the explanations we offer, and are seen to be involved in a great many different natural processes. A theoretical entity that had only one role in explanation, e.g. to conserve energy in some specific kind of process, would be highly suspect. But one that has as many different properties as a copper atom does, and manifests itself in as many different ways as copper atoms do, cannot plausibly be supposed to be a theoretical fiction. The theoretical picture of modern chemistry, to which the theory of copper belongs, is too tightly interconnected for it to be anything other than what it purports to be.

The emergence of this scientific image of the world really has only one plausible explanation, viz. that the world is, in reality, structured more or less as it appears to be, and, consequently, that the kinds distinguished in it (the chemical substances, particles, fields, biological species, etc.) are natural kinds of one sort or another, and that the causal powers they appear to have are genuine. They may not all be natural kinds in the strict sense in which I use this term in *Scientific Essentialism*. But nor are they just arbitrary classifications that lack adequate foundations in the real world.[2] Any other hypothesis would make the appearance of all this structure in the scientific image astounding. The hypothesis that the appearance of structure arises from our manner of perceiving or thinking about the world has no plausibility at all. It does not even begin to explain the structures that we actually find in chemistry, for example. Moreover, the hypothesis that our mental processing systematically distorts reality in some way, so that the real structures are not the same as the apparent ones, is simply gratuitous. It explains nothing, and the doubt that the structures are as they are represented as being is merely sceptical.

This is the real argument for the proposed ontology of scientific realism. It is a powerful argument, and it is independent of any theory of reference or truth. It does not proceed from any premises about the truth, or approximate truth, of the laws or theories of science. Nor does it depend on any semantic theory about what makes a law or theory true, or approximately true. It does not even depend on our acceptance of the truth or approximate truth of most established scientific theories. It is enough if we accept that the scientific image is the most rational picture to have of the nature of reality. The argument by-passes all questions about the language of science, and gets down to the crucial question, which is: How is the emergence of a scientific image of the world, consisting of a multiply connected, hierarchical structure of categorically distinct kinds of physical systems that are involved in a range of categorically distinct kinds of processes, to be explained? What gives rise to this image? The image is clearly a human construct. But it is a stable and revealing image that

---

[2] Biological species, for example, are what I call 'generic cluster kinds'. See my reply to Stephen Mumford in Ellis (2006).

accommodates and explains just about everything in the relevant fields that scientific investigation has demonstrated, and excludes nothing that seems to be indispensable. This is what we should expect, if the new scientific image were, for the most part, descriptive of reality, as physical realism assumes it to be. Its emergence otherwise has no plausible explanation.

References

Bigelow, J. C. and Pargetter, R. J. (1990). *Science and Necessity*. Cambridge: Cambridge University Press.

Carnot, S. (1824). 'Reflexions sur la Puissance Motrice du Feu', reprinted in Magie (1935).

Ellis, B. D. (1976). 'The Existence of Forces', *Studies in the History and Philosophy of Science* 7: 171–85.

—— (1987). 'The Ontology of Scientific Realism', in *Metaphysics and Morality: Essays in Honour of J.J.C. Smart*, ed. P. Pettit, R. Sylvan and J. Norman. Oxford: Blackwell: 50–70.

—— (1990). *Truth and Objectivity*. Oxford: Basil Blackwell.

—— (1992). 'Scientific Platonism. An Essay Review of Bigelow and Pargetter's *Science and Necessity*', *Studies in the History and Philosophy of Science* 23: 665–79.

—— (2001). *Scientific Essentialism*. Cambridge: Cambridge University Press.

—— (2002). *The Philosophy of Nature: A Guide to the New Essentialism*. Chesham: Acumen.

—— (2006). 'Universals, the Essential Problem and Categorical Properties', this volume.

Magie, W. F. ed. (1935). *Source Book in Physics*. New York and London: McGraw-Hill.

Psillos, S. (1999). *Scientific Realism: How Science Tracks the Truth*. London and New York: Routledge.

Sellars, W. (1963). *Science, Perception and Reality*. London: Routledge and Kegan Paul.

Smart, J. J. C. (1963). *Philosophy and Scientific Realism*. London: Routledge and Kegan Paul.

CHAPTER 2

SCIENTIFIC REALISM AND METAPHYSICS

Stathis Psillos

1. Introduction

There are two ways to conceive of what scientific realism is about. The first is to see it as a view about scientific theories; the second is to see it as a view about the world. Some philosophers, most typically from Australia, think that the second way is *the* correct way. Scientific realism, they argue, is a metaphysical thesis: it asserts the reality of some types of entity, most typically unobservable entities. I agree that scientific realism has a metaphysical dimension, but I have insisted that it has other dimensions too. In my (1999), scientific realism is characterised thus:

> *The Metaphysical Thesis*: The world has a definite and mind-independent structure.
>
> *The Semantic Thesis*: Scientific theories should be taken at face-value.
>
> *The Epistemic Thesis*: Mature and predictively successful scientific theories are (approximately) true of the world. The entities posited by them, or, at any rate, entities very similar to those posited, inhabit the world.

These theses mesh scientific realism as a view about the world with scientific realism as a view about theories. They imply no deep division between the two ways of viewing scientific realism. Taking scientific realism as a view about theories is *not* metaphysically neutral. Yet, scientific realism does not imply *deep* metaphysical commitments. It does not imply commitment to physicalism or to a non-Humean metaphysics.

In 'Physical Realism', Brian Ellis takes my understanding of scientific realism to task. He takes scientific realism to be a view about the world and claims that taking it as a view about theories is wrong (and wrong-headed). He goes even further. He argues that scientific realism should be seen as a rich metaphysical world-view that commits its proponents to physicalism and non-Humeanism.

Though I think Ellis raises important challenges, I disagree with his overall perspective. I accept physicalism and am very sympathetic to Humeanism. But my prime concern here is whether scientific realism should be committed to any of these. I think it should not. These are important issues that should be dealt with independently of the issue of realism in general and of scientific realism in particular. This does not imply that there are no connections between these issues. But it is only when we put these connections into proper perspective that we see what they are.

To put my prime point in a nutshell, the tendency to take scientific realism to be a richer metaphysical view than it is (ought to be) stems from the fact that there are *two* ways in which we can conceive of reality. The first is to conceive of reality as comprising all *facts* and the other is to conceive of it as comprising all and only *fundamental facts*. I will explain these two senses shortly. But my diagnosis is that scientific realism should be committed to a factualist view of reality and not to a fundamentalist view of it. In the body of this paper I will explain and defend this view. On the way, I will argue that the concept of truth is required for a sensible understanding of the metaphysical commitments of scientific realism. I will also argue that an anti-fundamentalist conception of reality acts as a *constraint* on scientific realism, but that it is a further and (conceptually) separate issue whether or not a scientific realist should come to adopt a fundamentalist view of reality.

2. A factualist conception of reality

Ellis starts with a well-taken distinction between truth and reality. Truth is attributed to our *representations* of the world. Reality is attributed to the world. Yet, this difference does not foreclose a link between truth and reality. On the contrary, on the *factualist* conception of reality, that is that what is real is what is factual (reality being the totality of facts), there is a two-way traffic between truth and reality. Reality is the realm of facts (truth-makers)[1] and to say that a representation of it is true is to say that

---

[1]   Given the close link between propositions and facts, it's important to understand facts as the truth-makers of true propositions.

it represents a fact: we can go from truth to the facts and from the facts to truth.

This, we might say, is a *metaphysically loaded* conception of truth. Ellis favours a 'metaphysically neutral' conception of truth. He equates truth with epistemic rightness. But though cast in epistemic terms, this conception of truth is *not* metaphysically unloaded. Undoubtedly, judgements about the truth of a matter can (and should) be based on the empirical evidence there is for or against it. But judgements of truth are different from truth. The difference is already there in mundane cases, but it becomes forceful if we consider limiting cases. Suppose we are at the limit of scientific inquiry and claim that all evidence (empirical plus theoretical virtues) for the truth of a theory is in. Suppose we say this theory *is* true. When we reflect on this idealised situation, there are two possibilities. The *first* is that the ideal (epistemically right) theory cannot possibly be false. The *second* is that it is still possible that it is false. If we take truth to be an epistemic concept, it is no longer open to us to think of the second possibility as genuine. But this amounts to a certain metaphysical commitment permeating a seemingly metaphysically neutral conception of truth. The metaphysical character of this commitment becomes evident if we take seriously the second possibility noted above. It amounts to a possibility of a *divergence* between what there is in the world and what is issued as existing by an epistemically right theory, which is licensed by the (best) evidence or other epistemic criteria. I think this possibility captures in the best way the realist claim that truth is answerable to an independent world. (More on this in section 5). The pertinent point is that this is a metaphysical possibility (or a metaphysical thesis) and hence its negation (the first possibility noted above) is also metaphysical.

The foregoing possibility of divergence implies an evidence-transcendent understanding of truth. It might be argued, quite plausibly, that as a matter of fact, whatever is issued by an epistemically right theory is what *really* exists in the world. The realist can easily accommodate the envisaged possibility of convergence by taking the right side in the relevant Euthyphro contrast: Is the world what it is because it is described as thus-and-so by an epistemically right theory *or* is a theory epistemically right because the world is the way it is? At stake here is the order of dependence. Realists should go for the second disjunct. This move makes the world the determinant of epistemic rightness. But this move is not available if the conception of truth is epistemic. My first conclusion is two-fold. On the one hand, the conception of truth that Ellis favours is not metaphysically neutral. On the other hand, it is at odds with some basic commitments that realists should endorse.

I do not think that Ellis's project depends on his epistemic conception of truth. His main argumentative strategy stems from his claim that truth is not metaphysically transparent. To say that the proposition *p* is true is not yet to say *what it is* that makes it true. Or, to put it differently, it is not *ipso facto* clear what kinds of fact it commits us to.

3. A fundamentalist conception of reality

There is a kernel of truth in the claim that truth is not metaphysically transparent. To capture this kernel, let me introduce another way of conceiving reality (the first, recall, was the factualist way). We may think of reality as comprising only whatever is *irreducible, basic* or *fundamental.* Accordingly, reality can still be taken to be the realm of facts, but this is an *elite* set of facts. Under this fundamentalist conception of reality, the factualist conception of reality noted above is not enough to give realism. Some contested propositions are true; hence they represent *some* facts. But what facts they represent is *not* metaphysically transparent; they might represent different (more fundamental) facts than it appears. Differently put, truth is not metaphysically transparent for the following reason: a true proposition will represent some facts, but it won't necessarily represent them *perspicuously.* The very distinction between representing a fact and representing a fact perspicuously is the kernel of truth in the claim that *truth is not metaphysically transparent.* This line of thought leads to a bifurcation: one might take a reductive or an eliminative attitude towards a set of putative facts.

Let's start with reductivism, as a form of (or a vehicle for) fundamentalism. A reductivist is not, *ipso facto*, an anti-realist. She will be an anti-realist only if she believes that the reduced facts somehow *lose* their factual status. But this is not necessarily so. If reduction is identity or supervenience, the reduced facts do not cease to be facts. On the contrary, far from having their factuality contested, the factuality of the reduced facts is legitimised. If reduction is taken to *remove* factuality, then it amounts to elimination, which is a totally different story. If elimination is taken seriously it should not be taken to imply that some putative facts are reduced to some other facts. It must be taken to imply that reality is empty of these putative facts. An eliminativist might (and most typically will) grant that there are facts in the world but she will deny that these facts are the truth-makers of the contested propositions. At the same time, an eliminativist will not necessarily deny that the contested propositions purport to refer to facts. She will claim that they *fail* to do so, since there are no relevant facts. That is, she will claim that the contested propositions are *false*. An eliminativist might also find some *use* for these false propositions, but this will not alter the claim that they are false.

If reductivism is distinguished from eliminativism, we can be clear on what reduction achieves: it removes the *sui generis* character of some facts. So for instance, there are no *sui generis* mental facts, if the identity theory of mind is true. Similarly, there are no *sui generis* mathematical facts, if logicism is true. But from the claim that '7 + 5 = 12' does not represent a *sui generis* mathematical fact it does *not* follow that it does not represent a fact. Reduction does not show that something is unreal. It shows that it is not *sui generis*. Differently put, it shows (or supports the claim) that the contested class of propositions is metaphysically *untransparent*, not that it is *untrue*. So reductivism is *not* anti-factualism.

4. Factualism vs fundamentalism

The factualist and the fundamentalist conceptions of reality are *not* the same: they are not logically equivalent. One can adopt a factualist view without being *ipso facto* committed to the view that there is an elite class of fundamental facts (or a hierarchical structure of facts). One can be a pluralistic realist about facts. In fact, there is no logical obstacle in accepting that facts of a more fundamental level are suitably connected with facts of a less fundamental level, without thereby denying the reality of the less fundamental facts. The converse, of course, does not hold. Admitting an elite class of fundamental facts *entails* a factualist view of reality (though restricted to the truths about the elite class). But the difference between the two conceptions of reality suggests that there is need for an independent argument for the claim that facts can be divided into more and less fundamental or for the claim that the only facts there are the members of the elite class of fundamental facts.

I take it that fundamentalism acts as a *constraint* on one's conception of reality. The primary component of realism is *factualism*. But in light of the possibility that a set of propositions may not perspicuously represent the facts, a realist about them must start with an anti-fundamentalist *commitment*. She must take it to be the case that, until further notice, she deals with *not-further-reducible* facts. To put it more linguistically, before one reads off any metaphysical commitments from a true proposition, one must choose to take this proposition at face-value. This is a commitment (hence, it can be revoked) to take truth as metaphysically transparent *in the first instance*. So though there is indeed a kernel of truth in the claim that truth is *not* metaphysically transparent, one *can* start with a commitment to its metaphysical transparency, if one starts with a factualist conception of reality and a face-value understanding of the propositions employed to represent it. Then, a *conceptually separate* debate can start. If the contested propositions turn out to be metaphysically untransparent, then a realist will not cease to be a realist if she argues that their truth-makers are not those implied by a literal reading of these propositions, provided she also holds that these truth-makers *ground* the facts that were taken to be implied by the literal truth.

If we keep the distinction between factualism and fundamentalism in mind, a number of philosophical benefits follow. *First*, we can put the realism debate in proper focus: realism is about what is real and not about what is fundamentally real. *Second*, we can become clear about the metaphysical commitments that accompany a realist stance about a certain domain: there are genuine facts that make true the propositions of this domain. To say of a fact that it is genuine is to say that it cannot be eliminated from ontology. The right (realist) attitude for a given set of contested propositions is to start with a commitment that it *does* represent genuine facts and then to engage in the independent debate about whether they are *sui generis* or not. If it is shown that these genuine facts are not *sui generis*, if, that is, there are some more fundamental facts that render the contested propositions true, this might revise our deep metaphysical commitments but *not* our claims to truth and reality. *Third*, we can be realists about a number of domains (or subject-matters) without necessarily taking a stance on independent metaphysical issues. I would like to insist on the following point. The issue of whether some entities are basic, or derivative, or irreducible, or *sui generis*, is a *separate* concern and needs to be addressed separately. In general, it will stem from *other* metaphysical commitments that one might have, e.g., a commitment to physicalism, or naturalism, or materialism, or pluralism. *Fourth*, there is a clear sense in which one can be an anti-realist about a number of domains (or subject-matters). One will take the contested propositions at face value and *deny* that there are facts that make them true.[2] But an anti-realist need not be driven by a fundamentalist conception of reality. She need not think that the contested propositions are false because they fail to represent some *fundamental* facts. It is enough that they fail to represent any facts – more specifically, those implied by the literal understanding of them. Of course, someone might start with a fundamentalist conception of reality. But this would lead to anti-realism about a set of putative facts only if some eliminativist stance towards them was adopted.

Hence, though I agree with Ellis that 'the real work has yet to be done', I doubt that this real work falls within the (scientific) realism debate *per se*.

5. Mind-independence

Plausibly, realism has been taken to assume that the real is mind-independent. This is partly for historical reasons. Realism has been taken to be opposed to idealism, the view, roughly put, that whatever exists is mind-dependent because only mental stuff exists. I think idealism is best construed as a kind of fundamentalism and that its proper contrast is *materialism*. Berkeley was an immaterialist, after all.

Though I think that a kernel of truth in the realist claim of mind-independence should be preserved, we should be clear

---

[2] Of course, there is another way to be an antirealist. This is to say that the propositions of the contested class are not *really* propositions: they are not apt for truth and falsity; they cannot admit of truth-values. Traditional syntactic instrumentalism, ethical noncognitivism and mathematical formalism might be classified under this view. I would call this view non-factualism (since the contested propositions are said not to be in the business of describing facts) and I would distinguish it from anti-factualism (which says that the contested propositions are *false*). But I will not discuss non-factualism further. For an important attempt to describe and challenge the metaphysics of non-factualism, see Devitt (2001).

about what this kernel is. It is not helpful to understand mind-independence in terms of some descriptions that facts should satisfy (or in terms of some characteristic that they may possess). That is, to describe the facts as physical (or material) or as non-mental does not help us understand what it is for them to be mind-independent. In support of this, let us consider the case of modern verificationists. They do *not* doubt that middle-sized objects exist and are irreducibly physical. Yet, they render their reality mind-dependent in a more sophisticated sense: what there is in the world is determined by what can be known (verified, warrantedly asserted) to exist. At stake is a *robust* sense of objectivity, viz., a conception of the world as the arbiter of our changing and evolving conceptualisations of it. It is this sense of objectivity that realism honours with the claim of mind-independence. The world is conceived as comprising the truth-makers of our propositions (allowing, of course, for the possibility that there are truth-makers for which we don't have, and may not have, truth-bearers).

How then should the claim of mind-independence be cast? It should be understood as logical or conceptual independence: what the world is like does not logically or conceptually depend on the epistemic means and the conceptualisations that are used to understand it. As noted already in section 2, this implies a commitment to the possibility of a *divergence* between what there is in the world and what is issued as existing by a suitable set of conceptualisations, epistemic practices and conditions. Modern verificationist views preclude this possibility of divergence by accepting an epistemic conception of truth. Can realists capture the kernel of mind-independence without taking a stand on the issue of truth? I doubt it, for reasons already canvassed by Taylor (1987). If I am right in my suggestion, truth is required for realism. Realism, particularly the independence dimension in it, cannot be properly stated without reference to a non-epistemic conception of truth.

These points have an obvious bearing on Ellis's claim that realism is independent of (a substantive non-epistemic conception of) truth. Briefly put, there is no logical obstacle for a verificationist anti-realist to accept Ellis's physical realism if it is seen as issuing in claims about what exists. To ward off this possibility, a physical realist should appeal to the mind-independence of these entities (or facts, as I would put it) and, if what said above is right, this is best captured by means of a non-epistemic conception of truth.

Michael Devitt (1997), who, like Ellis, takes realism to be primarily a metaphysical position, has insisted on the claim that the doctrine of realism involves no theory of truth. What has been stressed above is that taking realism to involve a non-epistemic conception of truth captures the realist claim of mind-independence. Devitt agrees that realism involves this claim, but notes that this claim can be captured without reference to truth. He says that realists can simply deny '*all* dependencies of the physical world on our minds', allowing of course that there are 'certain familiar *causal* relations between our minds and the world' (1997: 306). This allowance of a causal interaction with the world is well-taken. Indeed, realists should presuppose it if they want to defend the possibility of knowledge of the physical world. My objection to Devitt's point is that, even if it were granted that it avoided the concept of truth in characterising realism about the *physical* world, it cannot characterise the realist stance *in general*. Someone who is a realist about morality, for instance, might concede that moral principles wouldn't exist if people with minds did not exist. So she might concede that there is a sense in which moral principles depend on minds. Yet, she could still be a realist if she thought in terms of the foregoing possibility of a divergence between what we (or people, or communities) take (even warrantedly) moral principles to be and what these moral principles are. Casting this possibility of divergence in terms of a non-epistemic conception of truth about moral principles (alongside with an acceptance of the right side in the relevant Euthyphro contrast) would secure her realism (that is, the claim that moral principles answer to some moral facts) and, with it, a certain plausible understanding of the claim that moral principles are mind-independent.[3]

But can we grant that Devitt's claim avoids the concept of truth in characterising realism about the *physical* world? Devitt's realism implies certain existential commitments, and nothing more. His common-sense realism implies that cats exist, and tables exist, etc.

---

[3] Indeed, Devitt (2001: 591–2) has recently come very close to accepting a role for a substantive notion of truth in the characterisation of realism. It concerns what he calls 'atypical realism', the view that there are facts that make a set of propositions true but that these facts are not further explainable (or grounded). I claim that the general characterisation of realism must be broad enough to allow 'atypical' realists to be realists without any guilt.

His scientific realism implies that electrons exist and quarks exist, etc. Though existential assertions *are* existentially committing, there is an ambiguity in claims such as 'electrons exist'. The ambiguity does not concern electrons but *existence*. As noted above, a modern verificationist can (and does) accept that electrons exist. Their gloss on *existence* is that it does not make sense to talk about the existence (or reality) of electrons unless we understand this assertion to mean that . . . , where the dots are filled with a suitable epistemic/conceptual condition. Putnam's favourite replacement of the dots would be based on the condition of rational acceptability; Dummett's would relate to warranted assertibility; and Rescher's would relate to a cognisability-in-principle standard. Pretty much like realism, these views oppose idealism and phenomenalism. They entail (or at least are consistent with the claim) that material objects are real (be they the middle-sized entities of common sense or unobservable entities). The substantive disagreement between them and realism is bound to concern the *sense* of existence. In denying the anti-realist sense of existence, it is not enough for Devitt's realism to claim that electrons exist independently of all conditions an anti-realist might specify. There might be an open-ended list of such conditions (with more of those to be specified). What matters to their being *anti-realist* conditions is not that they make existence dependent on something but that they make existence dependent on suitable epistemic/conceptual conditions. It is this *core* of the anti-realist gloss on existence that realists should deny and the best way of doing it is to build into their realism a non-epistemic conception of truth.

As Devitt himself acknowledges (1997: 54, 109), existential assertions such as the above commit to the existence of the *entities* they are about only if we take them at face-value. He might well be right in saying that taking them at face value does not imply that we endorse a full and developed semantic theory about them (cf. 1997: 51). It might be enough, as he says, to understand them. This is very close to the realist commitment mentioned above. But note that this commitment is not as innocent as it might seem. As stressed above, it implies that truth is metaphysically transparent *in the first instance*. So when I say that electrons exist, I take this to commit me to *electrons* and not, in the first instance at least, to something else. Semantics (and truth) enters the realist position from the front door, by issuing a literal understanding of the existential assertion.

6. What is scientific realism?

What it is to be a *scientific* realist? I now think that this question is not fine-grained enough to be *really* useful. I agree that by making a claim to *realism*, scientific realism must make a point about what there is. But how are we to understand the qualifier *scientific*? It refers to science, of course. But can we talk about science in general and what it commits us to? A coarse-grained sense that can be given to scientific realism is to say that it asserts the reality of *unobservable* entities: there are genuine facts that involve unobservable entities and their properties. But note the oddity of this way of putting scientific realism. I do not, of course, doubt that there are unobservable entities. But isn't it odd that the basic realist metaphysical commitment is framed in terms of a notion that is epistemic, or worse, pragmatic? This oddity can be explained by reference to the historical development of the scientific realism debate, and more particularly by the fact that some empiricists thought that it is problematic to refer to unobservable entities or that scientific assertions should be *epistemically* transparent by being made to refer to observable facts. These empiricist (mis)conceptions might explain why the scientific realism debate took the turn it did. But they do not justify thinking of scientific realism as having to do with the reality of *unobservable* entities.

Note also that, as it stands, the coarse-grained view of scientific realism does not commit a scientific realist to any particular unobservables. It implies only the claim that facts about unobservable entities are among the set of facts. To say something more specific, as I think we should, (say, about electrons or tectonic plates or genetic inheritance) we need to start with a more determinate view of reality. The issue is not really whether unobservables are real, but rather whether electrons, etc., are real. To start from a more *determinate* conception of reality means to start with scientific theories (or subject-matters, if you like). We should declare our commitment to take them at face-value and make a factualist claim about them (which amounts to arguing that they are true).

This can be done at two levels of generality. The *less* general level concerns individual subject-matters, say physics or economics or biology. This is where the debate should turn. What is it to be a realist about physics, or biology or economics? I will not try to answer these questions now. But the points I made above suggest that to be a realist about a subject-matter is to take a face-value factualist stance towards it. Specific commitments to the reality of electrons, etc., follow by virtue of the two-way traffic between truth and reality. It is then clear how one can be a realist, say, about biology without also being committed to fundamentalism. Biological facts *might* be reducible to physical facts, but a) this is a separate issue; and b) it does not entail that there are no biological facts or entities.

The *more* general level concerns scientific theories (or subject-matters) in general. The question is: what is it to be a realist about scientific theories? Here the only essential difference between the less general questions asked above concerns the *scope* of the question: it is addressed to *any* scientific theory. The realist stance is essentially the same: face-value factualism. Given this level of generality, the realist commitment is to the reality of the entities posited by the theories (whatever those may be).

If I am right in this, it is *not* an accident that scientific realism starts with theories and takes the course for which I have argued in my (1999). Perhaps it was unfortunate that I called the last dimension of scientific realism 'epistemic'. I was carried away by sceptical anti-realist attacks on realism. I would now call it: the *factualist* thesis. With this in mind, my characterisation of scientific realism summarised in section 1 is not far from what I now call face-value factualism. One of its attractions, I flatter myself in thinking, is that it separates the issue of realism from the issue of fundamentalism. Besides, if we take the above line, it transpires that the issue of (un)observability is really spurious when it comes to the metaphysical commitments of realism. What difference does it make to the factual status of claims of modern science that they are about unobservables? None whatsoever. The real issue is whether there are facts about electrons, and not whether electrons are unobservables. In a parallel fashion, the real issue is whether there are facts about tracks in cloud chambers and not that these tracks are observable.

Ellis notes that my argument for scientific realism is a two-stage one: from the empirical success of science to the truth of its theories, to the reality of the things and processes that these theories appear to describe. He raises some worries about the concept of truth (in particular about whether it can carry the 'metaphysical burden' bestowed on it by the above argument) and then suggests that there is a way to cut out the middle-man (truth) and offer a direct argument for the metaphysical thesis concerning the reality of the entities posited by science.

Let me first offer a *qualified* defence of my argument. I do not agree that I offered a two-stage argument. Instead, I offered *two* arguments. This is because I took seriously another version of anti-realism: sceptical anti-realism. Let's not quarrel about whether van Fraassen's constructive empiricism is really sceptical. The point is that there have been significant arguments challenging science's capacity to track truth. The argument from the underdetermination of theories by evidence and the pessimistic induction are the primary ones. Oversimplifying, their joint message is that the claim that scientific theories are true is not (never) warranted. Again oversimplifying, my argument from (novel) empirical successes to the truth of theories (in respects relevant to the explanation and prediction of these successes) was meant to block the sceptical onslaught. This is what Ellis considers as the first stage in my two-stage argument. But it is an independent (and distinct) argument. My current concern is not with the success of this argument (though I still think it is successful); just that it had a certain distinct aim. I admit that I *might* have taken the sceptical challenge more seriously than it deserves. But then I still think that the realist victory cannot be complete if the sceptical challenge is not met.

Yet, there was another (distinct) argument that I offered (and this corresponds to the second stage of what Ellis takes my two-stage argument to be). In fact, I offered a battery of arguments for the literal reading of scientific theories (against reductive empiricism and instrumentalism), for the claim that the realist conception of truth should not be epistemic and for the claim that truth issues in existential commitments. I will not repeat them here. Suffice it to stress the following. Strictly speaking, what scientific realism needs is the truth of the following conditional: if scientific theories are true, then the entities posited by them are real. Its antecedent, to be sure, requires a literal understanding of theories and a non-epistemic conception of truth. So, I took it that what realists need to do is defend *literal reading plus nonepistemic truth*. And that's what I did. It is then a separate and empirical issue (taken care of by my first argument) whether the antecedent of the foregoing conditional is indeed true. If it is, by *modus ponens*, we can detach its consequent. That's how I perceive the dialectic of the two arguments I offered and the state of play in the scientific realism debate.

7. How strong is the metaphysics of scientific realism?

The real issue between Ellis and myself is whether there can be an argument for realism that avoids reference to truth. So what should this direct argument for realism look like?

Ellis is very explicit:

> For the question that needs to be addressed is this: How is the sophisticated, relatively stable, scientific image of the world that is the result of the last two or three centuries of scientific work to be explained? Don't look at it theory by theory, I say, and seek to justify the ontologies of the most successful ones in terms of what these theories are able to predict. Look at the picture as a whole (2006: 11).

What then should we be committed to? Ellis says:

> The emergence of this scientific image of the world really has only one plausible explanation, viz. that the world is, in reality, structured more or less as it appears to be, and, consequently, that the kinds distinguished in it (the chemical substances, particles, fields, etc.) are, for the most part, natural kinds, and that the causal powers they appear to have are genuine (2006: 12).

I fully agree with the *type* of argument Ellis puts forward. In fact, I think it rests on the only workable criterion of reality. It is the *explanatory criterion*: something is real if its positing plays an indispensable role in the explanation of well-founded phenomena. I take it that it is primarily Sellars's (1963) criterion. Yet, there is a *difference* between the explanatory criterion and Ellis's argument. The explanatory criterion is permissive: it does not dictate the status of the facts that are explanatorily indispensable. Nor is it committed to a hierarchical conception of these facts. The explanatory criterion is at work behind well-known indispensability arguments. This is to say that reality is one thing, fundamentality is another. Differently put, it is one thing to say that x is real because it meets the explanatory criterion, it is quite another thing to say that x is *sui generis* physical, or abstract or mental. Ellis's argument runs these two things together. Otherwise, Ellis needs to offer an independent argument as to why *all* the entities the scientific image is committed to are physical. If there is such an argument, it is only in tandem with it that the explanatory criterion yields physical realism. Recall that physical realism is the view that the world is basically a physical world. As he says: 'It is a world in which all objects are really physical objects, all events and processes are physical, and in which physical objects can have only physical properties' (2006: 4). I happen to believe that this right. But this is not the issue we are discussing. Rather, the issue is whether this conclusion follows from Ellis's argument. I claim it does not. It needs an independent argument for physicalism.

Physicalism (for that's what physical realism amounts to) *can* be argued for independently. But it is, I take it, an important conclusion that it is independent of realism and of scientific realism in particular. Can we get an argument for physical realism from current science? Suppose we can. I see no other way of doing it, apart from taking current science (as a totality) at face-value and claiming that it is true. The argument would be something like this. Current science posits

> things belonging to an elaborate, strongly interconnected, hierarchical structure of categorically distinct kinds (of chemical substances, particles, fields, etc.), and involved in natural processes which themselves are organised in a natural hierarchy of categorically distinct kinds (Ellis, 2006: 11);

current science should be taken literally; current science is true; *ergo* these things are real.

In any case, I doubt that we can get a *direct* argument for physical realism from current science. Does biology imply that there are no *sui generis* biological facts, or does physics imply that *all* facts are physical? Perhaps, physics does imply that *all* entities are physically constituted. But a fact can still be biological if there are biological properties. And I doubt that physics *implies* that there are no *sui generis* biological properties. Or, does physics imply that there are no numbers? Hardly. Ellis claims that the move from truth to reality licenses the view that all sort of things are real (platonic numbers, geometrical points, the theoretical entities of abstract model theories etc.) but argues that 'there is no plausible ontology that would accommodate them' (2006: 7). Here one can turn the tables on him: doesn't that show that the physicalist ontology is too narrow anyway? To avoid misunderstandings, I too favour a non-eliminativist physicalism. But I disagree with Ellis that the case for it has been settled by his argument.

Things become worse, it seems to me, if physical realism is taken to include an essentially non-Humean metaphysics. Ellis claims that the physicalism of the 1960s needs to be supplemented in various metaphysically inflationary ways and takes it to be the case that the scientific image posits causal powers, capacities and propensities. But even if it can be accepted that the scientific image implies that all things are physically constituted, can it also be taken to imply that their properties are powers, that they have essential natures, that there is real necessity in nature?

The idea that scientific realism must imply some strong metaphysical commitments is fostered (at least partly) by the tendency to associate scientific realism with naturalism. To put naturalism crudely, science is the measure of what is real. If naturalism is taken in its extreme form (physicalism), the implication is that only the physical can be real. The first thing to be said here is that scientific realism is independent of naturalism. One can be a scientific realist and accept *sui generis* non-physical entities. The second thing to be said is that, though independent, scientific realism and naturalism are good bed-fellows. So the important issue is whether naturalism dictates any strong metaphysical views. If you are a naturalist you should take current physics and biology seriously. But does current science imply any commitments to essentialism, dispositions, universals, natural necessity and the like? To put the question differently: does science imply a non-Humean view of the world?

Note, first, an irony. Answering this question requires taking science at face-value. That is, it requires that science implies that there is necessity in nature, that there are causal powers, essential properties and the like. But even if this were granted, it would still remain open whether these are *sui generis* entities. As noted above, this is an independent issue. A scientific realist can accept, say, causal powers, but argue (separately and independently) that they are reducible to categorical properties of the objects that possess them.

There is not an inconsistency in believing in electrons and in Humean laws and in all powers requiring categorical bases. But it may be thought that scientific realism (or naturalism) is best viewed in tandem with a non-Humean metaphysics. For the time being, I want to remain neutral on this. I don't think science *implies* a non-Humean conception of the deep metaphysical structure of the world. If, for instance, we take the Mill-Ramsey-Lewis view of laws as offering an *objective* and *robust* view of laws (see my

2002: 292–3), then one can be a scientific realist, accept that there are contingent laws of nature and take the aforementioned view of them. Or, if one is a scientific realist, one *must* accept the existence of natural properties, but take these properties to be Lewisian natural classes. Or, if one is a scientific realist, one may accept that some properties are powers, but deny that they are ungrounded powers.[4] Or, if one is a scientific realist, one should take causation seriously but think that, ultimately, it is a relation of probabilistic dependence among event-types. Despite all this, I think a scientific realist can be open-minded in the sense that there may well be independent reasons to take a stronger (non-Humean) view of laws, properties, necessity, causation, powers and the like.

8. Loose ends

Ellis might have a point when he says that if the semantic thesis of scientific realism is taken strictly, it is false. He presents lucid arguments against commitments to numbers, geometrical points, forces and theoretical ideals (such as Carnot engines). He claims that since theories, taken at face-value, imply their existence (if true), and since these things are not real, a face-value reading of theories should be rejected. To put his point more positively, a face-value reading of theories is not discriminating enough to tell us what we should be committed to.

I will not address separately each of the cases Ellis discusses. The *general* point that needs to be made is that the suggested face-value reading of scientific theories is a principled claim: scientific theories *can* be true or false and their truth-makers need not be any others than those implied by the literal reading of these theories. This is *not* to say that a scientific realist should be committed to the reality of everything implied by a scientific theory. Commitment to *most* of the entities posited by theories is enough. The real issue, then, is how the line is drawn. There might be a *principled* way to draw this line, but I doubt that this is part of scientific realism itself. This principled way corresponds to taking a stand in related (but distinct) metaphysical issues. If only physical entities can be real, then numbers (as abstract entities) cannot be real. If only actual things can be real, then theoretical

---

[4] In my (2005) I claim that current science does not commit us to the view that the properties of the fundamental particles are ungrounded powers.

ideals (such as Carnot engines) cannot be real. These conceptions of reality are not necessarily the ones that a scientific realist ought to have. They are independent and independently motivated.

There is, I think, a deep problem in trying to fix our ideas on a very definite conception of what is real. Seen from within, that is from the perspective on the world opened up by our theories of it, the issue we are discussing amounts to this: which of our representations represent facts perspicuously and which do not? An external answer to this question would require some *independent* access to the facts. If we knew already that there were no numbers (as platonic entities) or that there were no ideal entities (such as Carnot engines), or if we knew already that the only facts there were are physical, then we could dismiss some representations of them as non-perspicuous. But I don't thing there is such a thing as independent access to the facts. I don't mean to imply that facts cannot be known, or worse, that they are somehow constituted by our representations of them. My claim is much more banal. It is that before we raise the distinction between perspicuous and non-perspicuous representations of facts we need to take a stand on what putative facts are indeed facts and what putative facts are impostors. But given that they do not have these characters inscribed on them, we need some criterion to help us decide. My point then is two-fold. First, the best criterion available is the explanatory criterion noted above. And this, as we have seen, does not dictate a physicalist conception of facts. Second, even if we were to take another criterion of reality (e.g., that a real object is 'anything that has energy, or consists of things that have energy') this would need to be independently motivated. Someone might cease to be a physicalist if she does not accept it, but I don't see why she would thereby cease to be a scientific realist.

The issues that Ellis raises can be dealt with more *locally*. I will restrict my attention to theoretical ideals. In most cases, most typically in the case of Carnot's engine, we do have some *local* independent criteria to take them as fictitious. It is that the concept of a Carnot engine is so built that it can have no worldly *exact* counterpart. If the real world is the way science describes it to be, there cannot be worldly *exact* counterparts of the Carnot engine. This was known to Carnot himself, as well as to anybody else, and this knowledge is independent of the theory one (say Carnot) might use to explain the workings of a Carnot engine. I think this knowledge is enough to justify taking the Carnot engine to be a theoretical fiction. It's not the fact that the Carnot engine does not possess energy that makes it a fiction. After all, if it existed in nature, it would possess energy. Rather, more local and independent reasons suggest its fictitious character. But this does not imply that one cannot take literally *other* parts of the theory in which (descriptions of) the Carnot engine is embedded. Nor does it imply that one cannot take literally the theoretical description of the Carnot engine. After all, if one does not do the latter, one cannot explain why this theoretical fiction is so useful. It is useful because some worldly engine can be an *inexact* counterpart of the Carnot engine. *Inexact* counterparts of the Carnot engine are less efficient than it (that is, from the efficiency a Carnot engine would have, were it real), but their efficiency is independent of the nature of the working substance and dependent on the temperature limits through which they operate, just as the (description of) Carnot engine predicts.

The problem that Ellis raises for scientific realism is an important one. It is not always the case that entities implied by a face-value factualist view of scientific theories are real (worldly) entities. This puts the pressure on realists to show which of them are and which are not. But two things need to be noted in response to Ellis. First, realists need not steal the scientists' prerogative in this matter. It is they who tell us (the lay people) that Carnot engines and ideal gases are (useful) fictions, but electrons and DNA replication are not. Second, realists need to insist only on the (philosophical) claim that there is no reason to take *all* scientific posits as fictions and *all* scientific facts as impostors. This is, ultimately, what face-value factualism ensures.[5]

References

Devitt, Michael (1997). *Realism and Truth*. Princeton: Princeton University Press.
—— (2001). 'The Metaphysics of Truth', in *The Nature of Truth*, ed. M. Lynch. Cambridge, MA: MIT Press.
Ellis, Brian (2006). 'Physical Realism', this volume.
Psillos, Stathis (1999). *Scientific Realism: How Science Tracks Truth*. London: Routledge.
—— (2002). *Causation and Explanation*. Acumen & McGill-Queens University Press.
—— (2005). 'What do Powers do when they are not Manifested?', *Philosophy and Phenomenological Research*, in press.
Sellars, Wilfrid (1963/1991). *Science, Perception and Reality*. Atascadero CA: Ridgeview Publishing Company.
Taylor, Barry (1987). 'The Truth in Realism', *Revue Internationale de Philosophie* 160: 45–63.

[5]   Research for this paper was funded by the framework EPEAEK II in the programme Pythagoras II.

CHAPTER 3

KINDS AND ESSENCES

John Heil

Brian Ellis defends a striking brand of realism he calls physical realism (Ellis 2001, 2002). Traditional scientific realism takes as its starting point the success of the scientific enterprise. How better to explain this success than by supposing scientific theories are true? This modest suggestion is extended to the meatier thesis that scientific theories – at any rate the successful theories – are to be taken at face value. Such an attitude encourages the thought that a realist must endorse an ontology that includes, in addition to genes and electrons, numbers, sets, spatial points, and ideal gases.

Ellis urges us to move beyond the thought that all there is to realism is the flat-footed acceptance of scientific truths. An ontologically serious realist goes on to ask what the world must be like if our best theories are true. We accept mathematical truths and mathematical characterizations of natural objects and processes. Does this mean that a realist must accept the existence of mathematical entities: functions, sets, numbers? Do mathematical truths call for non-worldly truth makers? The physical realist's approach is vividly illustrated by quantum physics: it is one thing to embrace the quantum theory, another matter entirely to say what the world must be like if the theory is true.

Why should anyone care what philosophers think about such things? Surely finding out what the world is like is, if anything is, a job for empirical science. Here we do well to distinguish particular claims about how things stand – empirical claims – from ontological theses cultivated by philosophers. Ontological theses might be construed, in part at least, as attempts to make sense of the scientific story taken as a whole. The several sciences afford, not a single view of the world, but a patchwork of views. Knitting together the fragments is one distinctively philosophical task. Another is the development of a unified categorical framework within which scientific truths can be plotted. The endeavour is a priori, but not exclusively so. Ontological categories reflect rather than dictate scientific practice.

So many ontologies, so little time

Suppose we ask what sort of ontological scheme best accommodates the emerging sciences? Philosophers who think about such matters have tended to embrace what might be called a two-category substance–property ontology. Substances are *bearers* of properties; properties are *ways* substances are.[1] Theorists divide on the nature of properties. David Armstrong probably speaks for a majority in regarding properties as universals. Universals are shared, repeatable, entities (see, e.g., Armstrong 1989, 1997). Objects possessing the same property have something strictly in common: in Armstrong's enigmatic phrase, a universal is *wholly present in each of its instances*. Theorists influenced by Locke, in contrast, regard both substances and properties as particulars.[2] A substance is a particular object; a property is a particular way some object is. Properties as 'particularized ways' are nowadays called tropes (Stout 1930; Williams 1953; Armstrong 1978, 1989; Levinson 1978, 1980; Seargent 1985; Simons 1994; Heil 2003). On a trope view, you can speak of objects 'sharing' properties or possessing 'the same' property without embarrassment. Spherical objects *share* the property of sphericity in the way diners might share a fondness for anchovies; objects possess *the same* property in the way footballers might wear the same outfits. Here sameness boils down to exact similarity.

These points are worth keeping mind. They remind us that ontology cannot simply be 'read off' our ways of talking about the world. A conviction that distinct objects 'share' properties does not settle the nature of properties. In particular, it does not require that we regard properties as universals. This is Ellis's realist view applied to fundamental ontology.

Ellis (2001, 2002, 2006a) embraces universals and substances, but, unlike Armstrong, he defends a six-category ontology. The world comprises three kinds of concrete particular: objects (the substances), properties of these (tropes), and particular processes and events. Corresponding to each category of concrete particular is a category of universal: universals, instances of which are, respectively, objects, properties, and processes. The domain of universals

---

[1]   Martin (1980). Jerrold Levinson (1978, 1980) characterizes properties as ways; see also Seargent (1985).

[2]   Locke was simply expressing a preference for modes over universals shared by many philosophers in the Modern period, including Descartes and Spinoza.

is hierarchically organized. At the highest level are generic, maximally determinable universals. Determinants of these comprise the species. Being the mass of an electron is a species – an 'infimic species' – of mass, a determinate of the determinable mass. The mass of *this* electron is a particularized property: a trope.

Traditional universals – the kinds of universal favoured by Armstrong, for instance – correspond to Ellis's infimic species. Their existence depends on their instances. A world lacking electrons, a world in which nothing has the mass of an electron, is a world lacking the corresponding universal: if objects exist contingently, so do universals. Mass is an example of what Ellis calls the 'spectral universals'. Generic mass encompasses a spectrum, a continuum of specific masses. But, while you might think of the mass of an electron as a universal in some sense *made up of* its instances (particular masses of particular electrons), generic universals – generic mass, for instance – are not in any sense made up of determinate species of mass. Our world fails to include instances of every possible mass. This means that infimic species of mass will be gappy. Generic mass is, in contrast, continuous, not gappy.

We have mass, we have infimic species of mass – maximally determinate universals – and we have instances of these universals – maximally determinate tropes. Infimic species depend on their instances, but generic, determinable universals do not depend, or at least do not depend in the same way, on their determinates.

This picture is meant to extend to objects (substances) and to processes. Generic particles and processes occupy the highest level in the ontological hierarchy. Species of particle and process fall under these, and instances of these are particular particles – particular electrons, for instance – and particular processes – particular dissolvings of salt in water. Species constitute the natural kinds. There are natural kinds of entity (the electrons), natural kinds of process (salt's dissolving in water) and natural kinds of property (being the mass of an electron). The system is set out in the chart below.

Substances	Events/Processes	Properties
Generic Substantive Universals	Generic Dynamic Universals	Generic Universals
Infimic Substantive Universals	Infimic Dynamic Universals	Infimic Universals
Substances	Particular Events	Tropes

The world is layered, hierarchical. Generic, determinable universals occupy the upper levels. Falling under these are the species: determinants of these determinables. Species have subspecies; determinants can themselves be determinables. The hierarchy's ground floor comprises the maximally determinate universals and their concrete instances. The business of science is to spell out features of this hierarchy by examining the instances. Laws of nature are not ingredients of the hierarchy, but truths holding in virtue of the hierarchy's components. $F = MA$, for instance, is made true by dispositional features of massy objects. The truth maker is not the collection of concrete objects possessing mass, however, but generic kinds of which these objects are instances.

Ellis rejects attempts to reduce kinds of object to complex properties. An electron has a definite mass, charge, and spin. The mass of an electron, along with its charge and spin, are universals in a traditional sense. You might think these combine to make up the complex universal, *being an electron*. Ellis prefers to think of electrons as instances of *substantive universals* (the scholastics' substantial forms). Consider a particular electron. The electron has a definite mass, charge, and spin. These are – 'in' the electron – tropes, instances of property universals. The electron *itself* is an instance of a distinct substantive universal. The electron's mass, charge, and spin are essential to it, a reflection of the nature of the universal it instantiates.

Mass, charge, and spin, like all properties of the fundamental objects, are powers or dispositions. In one sense, this is *all there is* to the electron: an electron is an object with certain intrinsic powers that ordain it with capacities to affect and be affected by other fundamental entities. The electron is not, however, a mere bundle of powers. An electron is a *possessor* of powers. Electrons *have* properties; electrons are not *made up* of their properties. In this regard, Ellis's is a traditional substance–attribute ontology. Substances are not, however, 'bare particulars' to which properties are attached. Particular substances are instances of substantial universals that include various non-substantial universals of necessity. Instances of substantial universals possess these properties 'essentially'. An electron possesses a particular mass and a particular charge *because* it is an electron. The electron's location, in contrast, is a contingent matter: the electron can change its location, but not its mass or charge.

An alternative picture

Ellis's scientific essentialist picture will appeal to philosophers seeking unity and order in the sciences. Is this the end of the story? Not if you have qualms about hierarchical realms of universals. To bring Ellis's brand of essentialism into sharper focus, let me sketch an alternative picture.

Suppose the world comprised objects distributed about in space–time. These objects possess properties in virtue of which they behave, or would behave, in particular ways. Objects' properties are not universals or instances of universals, they are what, in Locke's day, were called *modes;* what others, including Ellis, call *tropes.* Modes endow their possessors with particular qualities. Modes are qualitative. But modes are, as well, powers. Think of modes as powerful qualities. Objects in the envisaged world are similar by virtue of their possession of similar modes. Modes are similar – or not – *tout court.* Similar objects will behave similarly in similar circumstances because a condition on their being similar is their possessing similar modes; and mode similarity is simultaneously qualitative and dispositional.

Complex objects in the world we are imagining are made up of simpler objects. Characteristics of complex objects are unproblematically fixed by characteristics of their constituent parts and relations these parts bear to one another. From this distance we cannot tell whether our imagined world is granular – consisting of distinct objects arranged in space – or unified – consisting of one or more fields with distributed 'thickenings' corresponding to more familiar objects.[3]

The world as I have described it is close to Locke's world, a world containing only particulars: particular objects and particular modes of those objects. These particulars encompass endless similarities. In some cases, the similarities are especially striking. This is so for electrons. In other cases, the cats, for instance, the similarities, although genuine, are more muted.

Call the world so described the Locke world. Does the Locke world contain essences? Cats are essentially mammals; electrons possess a negative charge essentially. Although a cat could fail to be grey, a cat could not fail to be a mammal; an electron could

---

[3] If this is right, we are in no position to ascertain a priori whether familiar objects (human beings, trees, rocks, electrons) are, at bottom, substances or modes.

fail to be in Cleveland, but an electron could not fail to be negatively charged. Are there truth makers for these claims in the
Locke world? It would seem so. The truth makers include the cats
and the electrons, but they include as well, our concepts. (Play
along for a moment, and pretend that *we* inhabit the Locke
world.) Nothing that lacked a negative charge would count as an
electron; nothing that failed to be a mammal would count as a
cat.

Ought we to worry that this turns electrons and cats into mere
artefacts, purely conventional entities? Maybe not. Our cat
concept and our electron concept, in common with many of
our concepts, are products of ongoing scientific exertion. Neither
concept was invented by dreamers. Both concepts reflect
serious engagement with the world. Both concepts circumscribe
genuine mind-independent similarities and important worldly
divisions.

Does the Locke world include natural kinds? Electrons might
be thought good candidates for natural kindhood. In the Locke
world, this would have to be a matter of the electrons being both
naturally occurring and exactly similar intrinsically. We want to
say, in addition, that it is no accident that electrons are alike
intrinsically. Perhaps it is enough to note that the intrinsic properties of electrons are evidently made for one another.[4] If a particle is an electron, it is going to be very difficult to make that
particle relinquish its negative charge. This might be possible if
we smash the particle in a synchrotron. If we do this, of course,
we destroy the electron. This truth holds in Locke's world as well
as Ellis's.

What the Locke world lacks is the kind of top–down unity
afforded by the apparatus of universals. Still, scientists in this
benighted world make do. They uncover deep similarities, which
are reflected in their formulations of what they unselfconsciously
call laws and explanations. These scientists are fond of explanation by decomposition. Faced with a complex phenomenon, they
endeavour to discover how the phenomenon might have been
expected given its constituents and their arrangement. All the
while they assume that similar things are similar, not merely qualitatively, but dispositionally as well. They sometimes put this
crudely by noting that objects that did not behave similarly in

---

[4] See Boyd (1991); and see Stuart (1999) for a perceptive discussion of Locke and
natural kinds.

similar circumstances would not *be* similar. The philosophers regard this as hilariously inadequate; the scientists regard the philosophers' sense of humour as distinctly off-key.

One question is whether resources adequate to describe the Locke world are adequate for our own world. Consider the fact that crimson objects are both red and coloured. In the Locke world there are no universals corresponding to the predicates 'is red' and 'is coloured'. Coloured objects possess maximally determinate colours. Suppose an object, *o*, is crimson. In virtue of being crimson, *o* answers to the predicate 'is crimson'. Does this mean that, in the Locke world, nothing is red, nothing is coloured? No. In virtue of being crimson, *o* satisfies the determinable predicates 'is red' and 'is coloured'. Three truths, one truth maker.

Does this undercut the generality of scientific theory? Why should it? Truths expressed by means of determinable predicates will still hold. They will hold, not because they concern determinable universals, but because they are satisfied indifferently by a family of dispositionally (and qualitatively) similar determinate properties.

Two difficulties

Ellis holds that an appropriately realist ontology needs a multi-tiered edifice of universals. But the edifice has its embarrassing aspects. Let me briefly mention two of these.

First, consider Armstrong-style universals. These are wholly present in each of their instances. What this could mean is far from clear, but, that mystery aside, it is easy to see how we could have epistemic access to universals so conceived. We are in causal contact with the universal in being in causal contact with its instances. This is because the instances are (is?) the universal.

Once we separate universals from their instances as Ellis does, we lose the possibility of causal contact with the universals. More seriously, it is not clear what the envisioned universals are supposed to be or why we should care about them. The instances do all the work, the universals get all the credit. The difficulty here is a species of a difficulty attaching to any doctrine that seeks to explain features, especially modal features, of our world by reference to goings-on elsewhere. In this case the otherworldly goings-on belong not to alternative worlds, but to a realm of universals.

You might think it unfair to invoke this as a special problem for Ellis. Many philosophers are fond of universals. Perhaps the cumulative weight of these preferences overwhelms niggling worries about their intelligibility. Let us grant, then, the apparatus of universals, and consider its internal plausibility. To simplify the discussion, let us focus just on two components of Ellis's conception: (1) the relation of generic, determinable universals to their infimic determinates; (2) the relation of property universals to substantive universals.

Ellis holds that infimic – maximally determinate – universals depend on their instances. No such universal exists uninstantiated. Think of this as a kind of 'downward' dependence. These universals depend as well on more generic, determinable universals. The universal mass of an electron exists only if (a) particular electrons exist and (b) the generic universal mass exists. Think of the dependence of determinate universals on their determinables as a kind of 'upward' dependence.

The idea that determinate universals have both upward and downward dependence relations looks unstable. One way to dispel this appearance would be to suppose that the relation between determinates and their determinables – having the mass of an electron, for instance, and having mass – is a kind of part–whole relation. Having mass is *a part* of what it is to have the mass of an electron. Now we can see why every object that could be said to have a determinate mass could also be said to have mass.

The resulting view looks something like this. Maximally determinate universals depend on their instances. But, being in a certain way composite, they depend as well on their 'parts'. These parts include their determinables (and determinables of these determinables) plus whatever distinguishes them from their sister determinates.

All this makes formal sense, but you might have higher standards. Consider distinct maximally determinate mass universals. Each of these will include the generic universal mass. What is it for one universal to be a component of distinct universals? Is this an unreasonable question? Universals, after all, are multiply instantiable. The relation between determinable universals and their determinates, however, is not the instantiation relation, but something akin to the part–whole relation. The question is, how is this supposed to work?[5]

---

[5]   The difficulty here parallels one raised by David Lewis (1986) in a discussion of 'structural universals'.

If you are puzzled by this question, you should be equally puzzled by substantive universals and the property universals that characterize them. Determinable and determinate property universals must be in some way 'shared' by endless substantive universals. Here again we have the one-over-many problem transferred to the world of the one.[6]

Naked powers

Ellis holds that intrinsic properties of the fundamental things are exclusively dispositional. Electrons have a particular mass, a charge, and a spin, for instance; and mass, charge, and spin can be understood as powers possessed by the electron in virtue of which it behaves – or would behave – as it does. At the fundamental level, then, the world is a world of *naked powers*.

Nevertheless, Ellis contends, not every property is a power; some properties are 'categorical'. Shape, for instance, is not a power. Indeed none of the traditional primary qualities are powers: shape, size, and number are *quantitative* properties. A spherical object's sphericity is a matter of its constituent parts standing in appropriate relations. Relations, or at any rate spatial relations, are powerless. Giving a lump of clay a spherical shape is not a matter of adding a property to those present in the clay's constituents; it is a matter of arranging those constituents spherically. So arranged, the lump has the power to roll, the power to look spherical, the power to fit smoothly through a round hole of a particular size.

We start with the thought that genuine properties are exclusively dispositional, our world is a world of naked powers. We then move on to the idea that, although this is so for the fundamental things, ordinary objects exhibit familiar categorical properties: shape, size, number. On closer inspection, these categorical properties turn out to be arrangements of objects possessing only dispositional properties. This suggests that categorical properties are at bottom fictions: there are the fundamental things with their dispositional makeup, and there are relations among these. What

---

[6] E. J. Lowe (1998: ch. 8; 2002) defends a four category ontology of substantial universals, non-substantial universals (respectively, Ellis's substantive universals and infimic species), particular substances, and modes (tropes). Particular substances are 'characterized by' modes; substantial universals are 'characterized by' non-substantial universals. Modes are non-sharable, non-transferable features of particular substances and owe their identity to those substances. It is not easy to see how this could work for the 'characterizing' of substantial universals by non-substantial universals.

philosophers have regarded as categorical properties are really nothing 'over and above' these, no addition of being.[7]

This would be the converse of the traditional idea that the fundamental things possess exclusively primary qualities (shape, size, number); the secondary qualities are nothing more than arrangements of primaries. Berkeley and Hume worried that a world consisting of objects possessing only primary qualities was, if not quite incoherent, at least indistinguishable from a world of empty space.[8] Can you so much as conceive of an object that has a shape and size but lacks colour? Would a world comprising objects possessing just the primary qualities be distinguished from an empty world?

What of a world consisting of arrangements of objects possessing exclusively dispositional properties? Think of a line of upright dominos arranged in a circular pattern so that one domino's toppling topples the rest. Now suppose that *all there is* to a domino is the power to topple and to be toppled. It is hard to see how any toppling could take place because it is hard to see what would be toppled. Keith Campbell, in a discussion of Boscovich's metaphysics of material points, puts it this way:

> We meet here a notorious conundrum in metaphysics. Is it possible for anything to be constituted by nothing but causal powers? Whatever the answer to *that* question, I doubt very much whether it is possible for *everything* to be constituted by nothing but causal powers. But that seems to be the situation in Boscovich's system. When one point moves another, all that has been shifted is a power to shift powers to shift. . . . But powers to shift *what?* To be coherent, I consider that Boscovich's points must be somethings which have the power to shift one another. . . . Put it this way: we do not understand Boscovich's theory until we know just how a universe with exactly one material point in it would differ from a universe containing nothing at all. (1976: 93–4)

---

[7] In Ellis (2001), categorical properties are assimilated to relations. In Ellis (2006b), Ellis describes categorical properties as 'dimensions' of dispositional properties, and takes them to be 'second-order' properties, essential to their bearers. This is an interesting proposal, one that could be understood as narrowing the gap between the ontology of scientific essentialism and the ontology I associate with Locke.

[8] See Berkeley (1710, §10); Hume (1739, Bk. 1, Part iv, §4). I owe these citations to David Armstrong, who develops a similar argument along materialist lines in his (1961: ch. 15). See also Armstrong (1999, 2002); Campbell (1976: 93–4; quoted below); Blackburn (1990); Swinburne (1980); Foster (1982: 67–72); Martin (1997); and Heil (2003: ch. 10; 2004). Ellis replies to the argument in his (2002: 171–6).

The difficulty here is analogous to the difficulty of imagining a world made up exclusively of relations. Relations require relata; objects possessing powers to affect other objects require qualitative 'filling in' of some sort. One possibility is that the fundamental things include some mixture of intrinsic powers and qualities. Ellis's idea, if I understand him, is somewhat different.

First, Ellis might not regard a world of pure powers as in any way problematic. Second, on one reading Ellis allows for categorical – what I prefer to call qualitative – properties to *supervene* on objects lacking such properties and their relations. The world, then, the whole world including the fundamental things and their relations, *our* world, might be taken to include qualities. These are absent from the fundamental things, but present in objects we care about.

How is this supposed to work, how could the qualitative be built up from the non-qualitative? One worry here is that we are veering dangerously close to the venerable doctrine that the qualitative nature of the world resides wholly in the minds of observers. This doctrine, coupled with the thought that powers require qualitative clothing pushes us in the direction of the Berkeleyan idea that the world is at bottom mind-dependent.[9]

Suppose we agree to think of the world as incorporating a mixture of categorical – qualitative – and dispositional properties. Which are which? Ellis offers *shape* as a paradigmatically qualitative property. But if shape is not-dispositional, how could we perceive objects' shapes? How could have knowledge of a billiard ball's sphericity? Here is Ellis:

> Spatial properties, such as shape and size, are known to us because things of different shape or size affect us differentially. They produce in us different patterns of sensory stimulation, so that things of different shape and size look or feel different. They also behave differently, and different patterns of behaviour, such as rolling or sliding, are readily associated with different shapes. (2001: 136)

Talk of 'affecting' and 'producing' is causal talk. A ball rolls or would roll in virtue of its shape. A Rubik's cube looks or would look cubical because it is cubical. If sphericity and cubicity differentially affect the causal powers of their possessors, this might

---

[9] This *is* the aim of Berkeley, Hume, and John Foster in the pieces cited in the previous note.

be thought to qualify them as dispositional. Indeed, it is hard to know what anyone could mean by describing properties as powers beyond indicating that they differentially affect the powers of their possessors.

Once you start thinking of properties in this way, it will be hard to come up with examples of genuine intrinsic properties of objects that are *not* powers. *Pace* Ellis, such properties would be unperceivable by virtue of making no difference to the behaviour of anything.

Are we back to a world of naked powers? Philosophers partial to powers are apt to assume unreflectively that, if properties are identified as powers this exhausts their nature: if a property is a power, it is a naked power. This leads to concerns about the place of qualities in the world. Are qualities absent? Are they ingredients alongside the powers? Do they 'supervene' on powers and their relations? None of these possibilities is especially attractive. Consider an alternative: properties are at once qualities and powers. An intrinsic property of a concrete object is a *powerful quality*.

Reflecting the science of his day, Locke spoke of primary and secondary qualities. A common interpretation of this distinction makes primary qualities *qualities*, secondary qualities *powers*. A better interpretation takes the primary qualities to be powerful qualities. Bear in mind that the primary qualities are, for Locke, qualities possessed by the fundamental material things. It would be incredible to suppose that these qualities are powerless, inert. Objects' shapes, sizes, and densities determine how they behave or would behave.

What of the secondary qualities? Locke and his contemporaries apparently thought these could be ignored by scientists investigating the material world. Is this because, as one prominent philosophical tradition suggests, the secondary qualities are mind-dependent? The question misses the point. Secondary qualities are arrangements of primary qualities picked out partly, but not exclusively, by reference to their characteristic effects on conscious observers. In investigating the fundamental features of the material world, we can afford to ignore the secondary qualities, not because secondary qualities are observer-dependent, but because they are 'no addition of being'. The fundamental things have primary qualities. Arrangements of fundamental things, arrangements of objects sporting particular primary qualities, make up perceivable objects that affect our perceptual systems in characteristic ways. (Perception, incidentally, is an excellent example of the mutual manifestation of dispositions constituting our perceptual systems and dispositions of objects perceived. Perceptual awareness is constituted by these manifestations.)

Conclusion

Physical realism affords an important new perspective on the ontology of our world. We have, on the one hand, an austere world of material substances and processes that possess properties, some of which are essential to their bearers. On the other hand, universals provide unification and a grounding for the kinds of necessity exposed by scientific investigation.

My suggestion is that a realm of universals as conceived by Ellis creates more problems than it solves. An ontology in the style of Locke could be ontology enough.[10]

References

Armstrong, D. M. (1961). *Perception and the Physical World.* London: Routledge and Kegan Paul.
—— (1978). *Universals and Scientific Realism,* vol. ii: *A Theory of Universals.* Cambridge: Cambridge University Press.
—— (1989). *Universals: An Opinionated Introduction.* Boulder: Westview Press.
—— (1997). *A World of States of Affairs.* Cambridge: Cambridge University Press.
—— (1999). 'The Causal Theory of Properties: Properties According to Ellis, Shoemaker, and Others', *Philosophical Topics* 26: 25–37.
—— (2002). 'Two Problems for Essentialism', in Ellis (2002): 167–71.
Berkeley, G. (1710/1998). *A Treatise Concerning the Principles of Human Knowledge,* ed. J. Dancy. Oxford: Oxford University Press.
Blackburn, S. (1990). 'Filling in Space', *Analysis* 50: 62–65.
Boscovich, R. J. (1763/1966). *A Theory of Natural Philosophy,* trans. J. M. Child. Boston: MIT Press.
Boyd, R. (1991). 'Realism, Anti-Foundationalism and the Enthusiasm for Natural Kinds', *Philosophical Studies* 61: 127–48.
Campbell, K. (1976). *Metaphysics: An Introduction.* Encino: Dickenson Publishing Co.
Cohen, L. J. and M. Hesse, eds. (1980). *Applications of Inductive Logic.* Oxford: Clarendon Press.
Ellis, B. (2001). *Scientific Essentialism.* Cambridge: Cambridge University Press.
—— (2002). *The Philosophy of Nature: A Guide to the New Essentialism.* Chesham: Acumen.
—— (2006a). 'Physical Realism', this volume.

[10] This paper was written for a *Ratio* conference, 'Metaphysics in Science', convened at the University of Reading, 1 May 2004. Many in the audience made useful comments and suggestions. I am especially grateful to Brian Ellis, Alice Drewery, and Ann Whittle.

—— (2006b). 'Universals, the Essential Problem and Categorical Properties', this volume.

Foster, J. (1982). *The Case for Idealism*. London: Routledge and Kegan Paul.

Heil, J. (2003). *From an Ontological Point of View*. Oxford: Clarendon Press.

—— (2004). 'Properties and Powers', in Zimmerman (2004): 223–54.

Hume, D. (1739/2000). *A Treatise of Human Nature*, eds. D. F. Norton and M. J. Norton. Oxford: Oxford University Press.

Levinson, J. (1978). 'Properties and Related Entities', *Philosophy and Phenomenological Research* 39: 1–22.

—— (1980). 'The Particularisation of Attributes', *Australasian Journal of Philosophy* 58: 102–15.

Lewis, D. K. (1986). 'Against Structural Universals', *Australasian Journal of Philosophy* 64: 25–46. Reprinted in Lewis (1999): 78–107.

—— (1999). *Papers in Metaphysics and Epistemology*. Cambridge: Cambridge University Press.

Lowe, E. J. (1998). *The Possibility of Metaphysics: Substance, Identity, and Time*. Oxford: Clarendon Press.

—— (2002). 'A Defence of the Four-Category Ontology', in Moulines and Niebergall (2002): 225–40.

Martin, C. B. (1980). 'Substance Substantiated', *Australasian Journal of Philosophy* 58: 3–10.

—— (1997). 'On the Need for Properties: The Road to Pythagoreanism and Back', *Synthese* 112: 193–231.

Moulines, C. U. and K. G. Niebergall, eds. (2002). *Argument und Analyse*. Paderborn: Mentis Verlag.

Seargent, D. A. J. (1985). *Plurality and Continuity: An Essay In G F. Stout's Theory of Universals*. The Hague: Martinus Nijhoff.

Simons, P. (1994). 'Particulars in Particular Clothing: Three Trope Theories of Substance', *Philosophy and Phenomenological Research* 54: 553–75.

Stout, G. F. (1930). *Studies in Philosophy and Psychology*. London: Macmillan.

Stuart, M. (1999). 'Locke on Naturtal Kinds'. *History of Philosophy Quarterly* 16: 277–96.

Swinburne, R. G. (1980). 'A Reply to Shoemaker', in Cohen and Hesse (1980): 316–17.

Williams, D. C. (1953). 'On the Elements of Being', *Review of Metaphysics* 7: 3–18, 171–92. Reprinted as 'The Elements of Being' in Williams (1966): 74–109.

—— (1966). *Principles of Empirical Realism*. Springfield: Charles C. Thomas.

Zimmerman, D. W., ed. (2004). *Oxford Studies in Metaphysics*, vol. 1. Oxford: Oxford University Press.

CHAPTER 4

KINDS, ESSENCES, POWERS

Stephen Mumford

1. Introduction: a basic sketch

Essentialism can be applied to a variety of philosophical problems, some of which are the central metaphysical topics of natural
kinds, causation and laws of nature. However, it is not perfectly
clear, I will argue, what the new essentialist is asking us to accept.
It cannot just be that there are natural kinds and causal powers
as it seems intelligible to accept these items into one's ontology
without taking the further step to essentialism. It is not even
obvious what such a further step will consist in. If it is an assumption about the properties of kind members, then it is not clear
what more the essentialist wants than that each kind-member
instantiates the appropriate properties, but this is something even
the non-essentialist can allow, as a case I call the universal accidental shows. The essentialist, it seems, must be asking us to
accept the Kripke-Putnam position, where the theory of direct
reference is extended to natural kinds. The problem with this is
that there seems to be no valid argument for acceptance of the
Kripke-Putnam position, at least if Salmon's (1982) analysis is
right. Is there some other reason for accepting Kripke-Putnam
essentialism, which is short of deductive certainty but nevertheless persuasive? Ellis offers such a reason: an *argument by display.*
Arguments like this are common in metaphysics. The argument
suggests a kind of cost-benefit analysis in which the start up costs
of a metaphysics are its basic assumptions and the benefits are the
enlightening accounts of various troublesome phenomena that
those assumptions are able to deliver. A good metaphysics will be
inflationary or wealth-creating, we might think. This would mean
that we would get more out of the theory than we have to put in.
However, I argue that it is not obvious that essentialism is wealth-
creating. The extra something that we must assume in order to
give us an adequate theory of essentialism may be precisely the
same as the putative benefits of the theory. It is not clear, therefore, that the essentialist assumption does produce a real gain.
The argument by display would not then be compelling.

I suggest that there is not yet sufficient attraction in the theory for us to accept the New Essentialism. We can still accept an ontology of causal powers; and a plausible non-essentialist account of natural kinds is also available. I am not yet offering an anti-essentialist position, however. There is no disproof of the theory. But I argue that essentialists still have work to do before we are obliged to accept their account of things.

2. The new essentialism

The best place to start is with Brian Ellis's recent contributions to metaphysics (Ellis 2001, 2002). Ellis argues that there is a new movement in philosophy, which he calls the New Essentialism, and includes Shoemaker, Martin, Molnar, Heil and Cartwright among its members (2002: 7).

The movement can be characterised by its negative and positive aspects. The negative aspect of the programme is a devastating attack on the old metaphysic of passivism. Passivism is represented by the Humeans who hold that particulars (usually understood to be *events*, in their ontology) are causally inert and bear no intrinsic necessary connections to each other (Ellis 2001: 7). Any connections that Humeans or neo-Humeans permit will be contingent, such as laws of nature traditionally understood. These are not a brand of necessary connection. The laws will merely be about or summarise the regularities that can be found to occur between types of events. One of the achievements of Ellis's analysis is to show that even some professed anti-Humeans, notably David Armstrong, retain a Humean basis of discrete and inert particulars and their systems fail when they attempt to impose anti-Humean necessity on top of a Humean, essentially contingent, basis. I find Ellis's analysis of the shortcomings of Humeanism an unqualified success and I have used it as a starting point in presenting my own version of anti-Humean metaphysics (Mumford 2004). I am in full agreement, therefore, with the negative aspect of the New Essentialism.

What, though, of the positive characterisation of the theory? At first essentialism is characterised as a belief in the *intrinsic causal powers* of things (2002: 1) but later are added *natural kinds* (p. 2) and then *essences* (p. 4). A theory of the laws of nature emerges in which the laws are metaphysically necessary. Laws are said to concern the essential properties of natural kinds. They could not, therefore, be otherwise. For example, the natural electron kind has the essential property of being negatively charged. This could not be otherwise because if anything were not negatively charged it would not be an electron. It qualifies as a law because of its necessity, which thereby supports inductive inferences and counterfactuals, as we believe laws should. One challenge to this account is that the laws of nature cannot be necessary because one can imagine a possible world with electrons that are not negatively charged. But this objection carries no force as imaginability is not a reliable test of possibility (Mumford 2004: 52–4). Whatever it is that one is imagining is positively charged in such a world, it is not electrons but something else: positrons perhaps.

That the world contains *de re* necessity is a contentious matter but not one that I will argue for here.[1] This paper focuses on a different problem: the notion of essence or essential property, which the New Essentialism claims as a source of such necessity. It is this notion that I think remains relatively obscure and for which I duly have reluctance to commit. Because I cannot commit to this clearly important component of the positive programme, I cannot yet be an essentialist. I cannot therefore be added to the list of new essentialists that Ellis presents. Nevertheless, I accept the intrinsic causal powers (Mumford 1998, 2004) and even natural kinds, suitably detached from essences, so I have something in common with the New Essentialism. Indeed, closer examination of the works of those cited in Ellis's list reveals very little mention of essences or essential properties. Most of them are included, it seems, because of their anti-Humeanism – the negative programme – and their acceptance of intrinsic causal powers. This makes me suspect that if they should be on Ellis's list so should I. But my preferred reading is that I shouldn't be on his list and nor should they.[2]

3. What is essential to essentialism?

Although Ellis emphasises the commitment to natural kinds and to intrinsic causal powers, it is clear that neither of these are the key commitment of the essentialist theory. As I stated above, one

---

[1] I accept (2004: ch. 10) that the world does contain *de re* necessities but I am not persuaded that essences are their source.

[2] Molnar has a brief approving discussion of essentialism in his 2003, pp. 182–4, though his essentialism is merely methodological: he accepts that essentialism is an assumption made in science. Cartwright makes no mention of essence or essential properties in her 1983 and 1989 and nor does Shoemaker in his 1984.

could accept either or both natural kinds and causal powers without being an essentialist. Neither is, nor are both together, sufficient to give us essentialism. This view is not universally accepted, however. In one study of natural kinds we find the view that 'the notion of a natural kind must first be tied to that of a real essence, understood as a property or set of properties both necessary and sufficient for membership of the kind' (Wilkerson 1995: 30). This sets a challenge for any non-essentialist who wishes to maintain that there are natural kinds. There are, of course, anti-essentialists who also deny the objective reality of natural kinds, such as Quine (1969). Dupré (1993) also denies essentialism and is so promiscuous about natural kinds as to practically deny them. Saying that every collection is a natural kind is practically the same as saying that no collection is a natural kind. Could we, in contrast, deny essences and uphold kinds?

One hope is that Ellis is able to argue for the existence of natural kinds before he introduces essences into his account. His initial argument is the *no continuum argument*:

> The distinctions between the chemical elements, for example, are real and absolute. There is no continuum of elementary chemical variety which we must arbitrarily divide somehow into chemical elements. The distinctions between the elements are there for us to discover, and are guaranteed by the limited variety of quantum mechanically possible atomic nuclei. (Ellis 2001: 3)

This is, of course, a decidedly a posteriori argument and the lack of continuum is presumably a purely contingent matter of fact. Hence the existence of natural kinds is a contingent matter. Far from being a difficulty for a theory of natural kinds, however, I will in due course argue that this is an advantage. A theory of natural kinds should allow that it is contingent which natural kinds there are and, therefrom, contingent that there are any natural kinds at all.

The critiques of essentialism from Quine, Dupré, and also Mellor (1977) come from a broadly empiricist tradition. But they ask a question of essentialism that even an anti-empiricist can take seriously. What is it that justifies elevating the status of a characterising property of a kind to an essential property? All that we could discover of a kind empirically is a property or properties that every kind member instantiates. This seems to be all that would be required for the *no continuum argument* to work. But essentialism requires more than just a property or properties that every kind member instantiates, and this is not, it seems, an empirical fact. To be essential, a property must be instantiated by every kind member, plus have some extra feature, as I will describe below. This is the *essential problem*: what justifies a property's elevated status of being essential to a kind? The essentialist needs to provide two things. First they should provide an account of this extra feature – of what it is – because it appears to be beyond the empirically discoverable characteristic properties of a kind. Second, they should provide an explanation of why it is rational to accept this extra something. Unless they can provide the account and the argument for its acceptance, we should believe in natural kinds only on the basis of the no continuum argument and therefore without a commitment to essentialism.

One might, therefore, be able to accept natural kinds without essentialism. In a similar vein, one can accept the existence of causal powers without accepting essentialism. Indeed many see an attraction to a causal powers ontology that is quite independent of any consideration of essentialism and natural kinds (Mumford 1998; Molnar 2003). Ellis himself leaves the connection quite loose, other than describing Humean and anti-Humean metaphysics in terms of whole packages of related claims. He thinks that some of the essential properties of natural kinds, given his anti-Humean acceptance of necessary connections, might be causal powers. These would account for the causal laws. But we are at liberty, I think, to accept the powers component of anti-Humeanism without adding the essentialism.

Some causal powers theorists, however, think there is a close connection between powers and properties. If they are right, there arguably is an essentialist commitment in the theory of powers. Shoemaker (1984: 210) argues that properties just are causal powers. This gives us a kind of essentialism about the causal roles of properties but it is, I argue, only a trivial essentialism that follows from identity. If a property P is constituted by a cluster of causal powers, c_1, c_2, c_3, then that property P could not be constituted by a different cluster of causal powers and still be P. As Salmon (1982) shows, however, essentialists typically want a more substantial essentialism than mere identity. Indeed, the New Essentialism seems to be more than just a claim about identity.

The account of properties as clusters of causal powers, which I defend elsewhere (Mumford 2006), gives us a clue as to how we might explicate philosophically our non-essentialist notion of natural kinds. This is because, following E. J. Lowe's (2002, 2005) work on the four-category ontology, natural kinds are best understood to be universals: substantive universals instead of qualitative or property universals.[3] Property universals, which Lowe calls attributes, can be understood as existing only in, and constituted by, the totality of their particular instances or modes.[4] How, then, should we think substantive universals or kinds are constituted? By their characterising attributes? I say not. Instead, and by parallel reasoning, I understand kinds to be constituted by the four-dimensional totality of their members. Kinds are just object types or object universals. Any essentialism that comes from identity will be, therefore, an identity between the kind and the class of its constitutive instances. There will not be an essentialist relationship holding between a kind and its characterising attributes, as the New Essentialism requires.

To understand this position, we need first to look at the substantial essentialism about kinds that Ellis professes to hold. We need to consider what the position is and whether there are compelling reasons to adopt it. I will claim that there are not and then go on to outline a non-essentialist theory of natural kinds.

4. Kripke-Putnam essence

I have argued that while the new essentialists are asking us to accept causal powers and natural kinds, they are not asking us to accept just those things. What are they asking us to accept in addition? It seems they are also asking us to accept the essences that are found in the Kripke-Putnam argument where the theory of direct reference is extended to natural kinds. This provides the necessity of Ellis's natural laws. The Kripke-Putnam position makes it metaphysically necessary that the natural kinds have their essential properties and it appears to be just such a metaphysical necessity that Ellis adds to his natural kinds. We find it in the following two passages:

> ... some things ... hold some or all of their intrinsic properties necessarily in the sense that they could not lose any of these

---

[3]   Ellis defends a six-category ontology, as John Heil describes and discusses (this volume).

[4]   This idea mainly draws upon Armstrong's (1978) immanent realism about universals.

properties without ceasing to be things of the kind they are, and nothing could acquire any set of kind-identifying properties without becoming a thing of this kind. These kind-identifying sets of intrinsic properties are the ones I call 'the real essences of the natural kinds'. (Ellis 2001: 237–8)

... it is a necessary truth that a thing of kind K has the property P if P is an essential property of K. It is, of course, a posteriori what properties are essential to a given kind. (Ellis 2001: 219)

Note that this is a specifically Kripkean essence as it appeals to metaphysical necessity. There have been other notions of essence, for example in Aristotle and Locke. But a Lockean nominal essence, for instance, would not be enough to yield the requisite metaphysical necessity of the New Essentialism. A Lockean nominal essence is a set of observable qualities of the kind. But Locke imports no metaphysical necessity to such essences.[5] The nominal essence of a kind could vary across possible worlds. Ellis could certainly not allow this as it would mean that his laws of nature were contingent only. He must adopt the Kripke-Putnam position, therefore, in which the relation between a kind and its essential properties is one of metaphysical necessity. This allows him to claim that, unlike the deniers of *de re* necessity, he thereby has a backing for inductive and counterfactual inferences: putatively one of the chief advantages of the new essentialist programme. But how strong, I consider in the next two sections, is the argument for Kripke-Putnam essentialism?

5. Reference and new essence

In the first place, I accept Salmon's (1982) analysis, which shows that Kripke and Putnam themselves do not have a conclusive nor compelling argument for essentialism about natural kinds. What Kripke (1972/1980) has is a theory of direct reference, and we can grant that this is a credible theory. But can it plausibly be claimed that a substantial theory of metaphysical necessity is derivable from the theory of reference? Kripke thinks so but it is mainly

---

[5]   In contrast, it has been argued that Locke's *real* essences do anticipate the strong metaphysical necessities of Kripke, see Mackie (1976: 93–100). In addition, they play an explanatory role for the nominal essence, which is said to flow from the real essence. For an account of this, see Fine (1994).

Putnam (1975) who does this work in respect of natural kinds. Putnam thinks that necessary, though a posteriori, truths about kinds can be generated by the *OK-mechanism*. This works in two stages, respectively providing reference and then essence:

O: refer to a kind-member *a* *O*stensively, where *a* has property F.

K: define membership of the *K*ind in terms of being the same as *a*, where this means having F.

I accept the sort of critique of this position that Salmon presents: who is to say (and how can direct reference theory say) what it is to be of the same kind as *this*, the subject of direct reference? The flaw of the *OK-mechanism* is that it builds in a conspicuously theoretical claim about the nature of kind membership. This is the essentialist claim that there is some property F that is metaphysically necessary for membership of *K*. Whether or not this is the case, it is not a claim that can be derived from the theory of direct reference alone; it is mainly a theoretical claim about kind-membership that has been taken as a metaphysical truth. There are many other possibilities. As well as having property F, *a* has other properties G, H and I. Why is it F that determines *a*'s membership of *K*, rather than G, H and I? Is F the only property that is common to all *K*-members? If so, why? If not, why is kind-membership not defined in terms of possessing G, H or I? And will there always be at least one property F that all kind-members possess? The essentialist position depends on definite answers to these questions but these answers are not derived purely philosophically. A theoretical view of kind membership must be added. That being of the same kind as *this* sample (of water) means being a sample of H_2O depends on the acceptance of a substantial scientific theory that being of the same kind is determined by molecular structure. While this is a view inspired by science, substantial essentialist commitments are added. Hence the claim is made that the kind-identifying property F is held by every kind member at all times and across all possible worlds. But such a claim is derived neither from the theory of reference, nor from a posteriori science, nor from the two together. It seems, therefore, that any essentialism to be found in the *OK-mechanism* is assumed rather than proved.

The above is not offered as a systematic refutation of the Kripke-Putnam position. It is intended to show that their attempt to derive essentialism about kinds from the theory of direct reference is problematic and, it appears, underdetermined. Their position purports to offer an argument for this kind of essentialism, which on examination looks more like an assumption of essentialism. The New Essentialism takes a stance on the essential properties of natural kinds that is as strong as the Kripke-Putnam position. But if my diagnosis, derived from the more detailed work of Salmon, is correct, then there is no compelling support for the New Essentialism to be found here. Indeed, this should come as no surprise to metaphysicians who, for the most part, would rarely, if ever, allow that a substantial metaphysical conclusion could be derived from the theory of reference alone.

6. The argument by display

Ellis's essentialism is of the Kripkean variety but Ellis does not invoke the Kripke-Putnam argument in support of his position.[6] If the *OK-mechanism* is deemed not to demonstrate such essentialism we cannot yet declare the New Essentialism a failure. Instead, Ellis attempts to justify his essentialism in the following way:

> The form of the argument is . . . an argument by display. You show your wares and invite people to buy them. If your system strikes your readers as being simpler, more coherent, or more promising than any alternative for dealing with the recalcitrant difficulties of other systems, then this may be a good reason to buy it. (Ellis 2001: 262)

The argument is, therefore, indirect. It does not qualify as the kind of a priori demonstration that metaphysicians may regard as the ideal. The reality, however, is that metaphysics often does proceed in this way. Lewis (1986), for example, offers no direct argument for there being possible worlds: it is the use we can make of them that justifies their acceptance. Similarly Molnar says of other putative realities: 'The compelling reasons for accepting the theory of powers outlined are in the work that the concept can do in one's metaphysics' (2003: 186).

The methodology that Ellis deploys is that of costs set against benefits. When we get down to matters of fundamental ontology

---

[6] Ellis does not rely explicitly on Putnam's argument in his 2001, though it is discussed approvingly in his 2002: 16.

in metaphysics, a subject in which questions of existence cannot be settled by empirical evidence, we have to find another basis for theory choice. What has emerged as a common methodology, as found in Ellis, Lewis and Molnar, is that one seeks a balance in one's fundamental ontology between economy and strength. One looks for the most economical set of assumed entities: the fewest types of basic entity, perhaps. But one also looks for a set of entities that will explain as much as possible of what we take there to be. An ontology that is very simple might not be able to explain enough. Empiricist ontologies typically take events to be their basic entities but then they are unable to provide the necessary connections that we take to be behind causation, laws and clearly successful epistemological practices. An ontology may be strong but uneconomical, as would be the case if we just allowed everything as a basic entity that anyone thought might exist. The most attractive ontology will strike the right balance between simplicity and strength.[7]

Ellis leans on such a view of metaphysics when he depicts us as market traders showing our wares to our potential customers. We are trying to show that our product is cheap for the benefits it will deliver. We may not have the cheapest ontology in absolute terms. Indeed Ellis would probably accept that the assumption his position requires – metaphysical necessities borne out of essential properties – is not as cheap a starting cost as empiricism. But empiricism cannot produce plausible accounts of laws of nature, counterfactual inference, and so on. Often the cheapest product on the market is not the best value. But the New Essentialism, Ellis would argue, is the best all-round package. Once its assumptions are accepted, so many of the traditional problems of philosophy will be solved.

I will be going on to criticise Ellis's claim that essentialism is a good overall deal. First, however, I want to discount a possible attack on the general methodology. It might be thought that such an argument by display would establish nothing more than which metaphysic is the most coherent but not which metaphysic is true. As the above explanation showed, we find only the system that achieves the best overall balance between simplicity and strength. But striking such a balance does not, we would ordinarily think,

---

[7]   Lewis's account of the laws of nature (1973: 72–7) made explicit appeal to this kind of balance between simplicity and strength. He sought the fewest possible laws from which most of the world's history could be derived.

entail truth. In the more general case, coherence is not thought to entail truth, hence a natural resistance to the coherence theory of truth. If the argument by display is all we have to guide theory choice in metaphysics, then it would appear that truth in metaphysics is nothing more than coherence. Because this seems to apply to all metaphysics, however, it cannot be fairly used to criticise the New Essentialism in particular. It may not establish essentialism as a 'strong' truth, where truth means correspondence, perhaps. But if essentialism is true only in the coherence sense of truth then it seems it is in no worse a position than any of the alternatives. Because metaphysics concerns the nature of reality beyond the appearances, it thereby has to accept certain limitations. Metaphysicians have relatively few tools at their disposal. Many of these are destructive, such as the reductio argument that can be used to show the untenability of a theory. When it comes to positive advocacy of a theory, the tools are even fewer. Favourable comparison of the costs of a theory with its benefits may be as good as it gets.[8]

The general methodology is not at fault, therefore. In the next section, however, I argue that even by this methodology, the credentials of the New Essentialism are questionable. In the first place, it is not entirely clear what the product is that the New Essentialism is asking us to buy. It is not clear, therefore, what the starting costs or assumptions of the metaphysic are. Second, I go on to argue that the most plausible analysis is that the starting assumptions must be identical with the putative benefits of the theory. In that case, the New Essentialism can hardly claim to be a good deal. The benefits it produces are not therefore real.

7. The cost and benefit of essentialism

For the argument by display, we must compare the price of what we buy with the benefits it procures. What are the benefits of adopting essentialism? According to Ellis, they are such things as a theory of immanent necessity, a theory of causation, a theory of modality and counterfactual inference, a warrant for non-extensional logics, and a dissolution of the problem of induction (mainly outlined in Ellis 2001, chapter 8).

---

[8] Ellis addresses methodological questions of metaphysics in 'Constructing an ontology' (forthcoming).

What price do we have to pay to gain all these benefits? This is where I think the New Essentialism is less clear. In the simplest terms, we have to accept that there can be essential properties of natural kinds. But what exactly is this assumption? It is not simply that every K-member have some property F. It has been demonstrated elsewhere (Mumford 2004: 116–18) that the universal instantiation of a property by every K-member is not sufficient to make that property essential for K. A property G is accidental for the kind K where it is contingent for any K-member k_1 whether or not k_1 instantiates G. k_1 might be G, therefore, and so might all other K-members $k_2 - k_n$. The essentialist is not asking us to accept, therefore, just that there is some property or cluster of properties possessed by every kind member. They must want us to accept something more. What is it?

I think that they are asking us to accept something quite complex. One thing we must accept is not just that all actual K-members instantiate the property F, but that all actual *and possible* K-members instantiate F. We are having to accept this as an immanent modal truth because a purported advantage of essentialism is that it provides modality without reference to possible worlds. If we accept that all possible K-members are F, then we are accepting that the counterfactual inference <if a were a K, a would be F> is sound. We are also accepting that unobserved (as well as observed) K-members will be F. Cutting to the chase, the concern here is that essentialism is not a wealth-creating ontology because the assumption that we will have to buy is *that* there is immanent modality, *that* there is a grounding for counterfactual inferences, *that* there is a grounding for inductive inference, *that* there are intrinsic causal connections, and so on. In other words, the assumptions that are needed to get essentialism started look like they are one and the same as the putative benefits. But if the benefits of essentialism are one and the same as the assumptions, an argument by display cannot count in its favour. We are only getting out of the theory what we originally put into it. The theory does not, therefore, have the property of being wealth-creating or inflationary that would make it look like a good deal. We cannot say that there is a favourable comparison of costs with benefits if the costs and benefits are the same.

This leaves essentialism in a relatively weak position. I have shown that there is no compelling philosophical argument for essentialism from the theory of reference. The Kripke-Putnam analysis fails. I have also shown in passing that there is no empirical proof of essentialism. All that can be discovered empirically is the characterising attributes for a kind (see Mellor 1977). That these attributes are, in addition, essential to the kind is not an empirical fact. The essentialist would have to find a principled reason why a characterising attribute was essential for the kind. If the analysis of the present section is right, the essentialist has not yet even shown that there is an argument by display in their favour. The theory does not appear to result in any benefits that we do not have already to assume. It cannot, therefore, lay claim to being a particularly good deal.

There is one remaining argument that might weigh in favour of essences, however, namely that no credible theory of natural kinds is possible without them. I take it that this is not the case, however, and in the next section I will explain how natural kinds could exist without essences.

8. Non-essentialist kinds

In a sense, there is no particular problem of natural kinds. Natural kinds are best understood as types or universals; hence the problem of kinds is a problem about universals. In the theory of universals, one of the most popular current theories, and the one to which I subscribe, is Armstrong's immanent realism (see Armstrong 1978). Universals and particulars are distinct and both real but, siding with Aristotle as opposed to Plato, universals exist immanently, only in particulars. In other words, a universal exists only in its instances. There is not some transcendent form that exists besides. Indeed, an uninstantiated universal would be no universal at all.[9]

Universals are most often discussed for the case of attributes. Hence the attribute or property redness exists only in its instances in red modes or, as some prefer, *tropes* of things. As the word 'mode' suggests, a mode is always a mode of some object. Modes cannot exist independently of an object that instantiates it, though nor can an object exist that instantiates no mode. The basic things that exist are objects-bearing-modes. Attributes are, therefore, *types* of modes-borne-by-objects. The universal-

---

[9] I follow Armstrong's four-dimensional commitment. Just one instantiation of a universal, at any place or time, is enough for the universal to be existent for all times.

particular distinction is merely an instance of the type-token distinction. A further naturalistic assumption often comes into play, which is that the world's modes naturally divide into types. For example, there is a naturally existing, mind-independent red-type of mode, which will be the universal redness. This is a really and wholly distinct type from greenness, squareness and many other mode types. There are some mode types from which it is not wholly distinct. The mode-type *being coloured* is a determinable relative to redness and the mode-type scarlet is determinate relative to it. The relations that hold between these overlapping universals can be understood in set-theoretic terms.

Just as there can be natural types of modes, which are the attributes, there can be natural types of object, and this is where we find a promising account of natural kinds. Natural kinds are simply types of natural object. (Artificial kinds would simply be types of artificial objects or artefacts.) They are types of objects-bearing-modes and again exist immanently only in their instances. Therefore, a natural kind with no members is no natural kind at all. Also like the case of attributes, the existence of each is contingent. This need not entail, however, that there could have been no natural kinds at all. Some philosophers think that there could not have been nothing at all, even though every single thing that exists is only a contingent existence (see Lowe 1998: ch. 12). If there has to be something, then there have to be attributes even if they have only single instances. Similarly this may mean that there have to be natural kinds, even if these only have single instances. A kind is not necessarily a group of resembling particulars as the notion of a unique particular, or one of a kind, is coherent.

Can this ontology avoid essentialism? It can because while natural kinds can be characterised by their attributes (horses are four-legged, have tails, manes, hooves, etc.), they are not constituted by those attributes. They are constituted by the omnitemporal totality of their member objects or particulars.[10]

The characterising attributes need not be essential to the kind. To form a kind, objects need only be of the same type, and all that will be required to be of the same type is resemblance. Resemblance requires only that there be common attributes. These can characterise without being essential. Indeed a universal but accidental characterising attribute serves just as well. This can be

---

[10] This view makes use of Lowe's four-category ontology, see Lowe 2002.

seen easily in the case where we have one of a kind. We would have great difficulty here in distinguishing the essential properties from the accidental ones, which would all be universally instantiated by every (the only) kind-member, in the nature of the case.

It might be objected by the essentialist, however, that even where two distinct properties F and G are instantiated universally by every kind-member, there can still be a counterfactual or modal difference between them. I may be able to say that *K*-members might not be G (in other words, there are worlds with *K*-members that are not G). However, I cannot say that *K*-members might not be F. This shows that F is an essential property for *K*-membership but G is only accidental. But why are there such prohibitions on our counterfactual inferences? There are such prohibitions, I argue, only on the assumption of essentialism for the characterising attribute F of *K*. The assumption of essentialism is all that backs one inference or modal claim and prohibits the other. This point exemplifies the claim of the previous section. One of the putative benefits of essentialism – the backing of counterfactual and modal inferences – is identical with the assumption of essentialism. This cannot, therefore, be an independently compelling reason for adopting counterfactual inferences as a way of distinguishing essential from accidental properties and thereby establishing that there are essential properties.

We are left, therefore, with a view of natural kinds as object types, existing only in those objects, just as a property or attribute exists only in its instances. These kinds can be characterised by attributes but a further assumption that any of these characterising attributes is essential is neither required nor independently motivated. A further pillar of support for essentialism has been removed, therefore. We do not need essential properties in order to have a credible theory of natural kinds.

9. Conclusion

The New Essentialism, if it really is a new movement in philosophy, must face the challenge of stating exactly what its assumptions are and what justifies them. These assumptions appear to be more than a belief in causal powers and natural kinds. Instead the notion of an essential property seems to be crucial. I have shown that we are still awaiting a compelling argument to believe that there are such things. Arguments are used that are short of deductive certainty though they nevertheless follow a methodology common in metaphysics. In this case, however, these arguments are not persuasive. It remains possible, therefore, to have an anti-Humean and realist ontology that still falls short of essentialism. I have not argued for this ontology here but I have argued for its possibility, a possibility which is effectively denied in Ellis's recent work.[11]

References

Armstrong, D. M. (1978). *A Theory of Universals*. Cambridge: Cambridge University Press.
Cartwright, N. (1983). *How the Laws of Physics Lie*. Oxford: Clarendon Press.
—— (1989). *Nature's Capacities and their Measurement*. Oxford: Clarendon Press.
Dupré, J. (1993). *The Disorder of Things*. Cambridge, MA: Harvard University Press.
Ellis, B. (2001). *Scientific Essentialism*. Cambridge: Cambridge University Press.
—— (2002). *The Philosophy of Nature*. Chesham: Acumen.
—— (forthcoming). 'Constructing an Ontology', in *Topics on General and Formal Ontology*, ed. P. Valore. Monza: Polimetrica.
Fine, K. (1994). 'Essence and Modality', *Philosophical Perspectives* 8: 1–16.
Heil, J. (2006). 'Kinds and Essences', this volume.
Kripke, S. (1972/1980). *Naming and Necessity*. Oxford: Blackwell.
Lewis, D. (1973). *Counterfactuals*. Oxford: Blackwell.
—— (1986). *On the Plurality of Worlds*. Oxford: Blackwell.
Lowe, E. J. (1998). *The Possibility of Metaphysics*. Oxford: Oxford University Press.
—— (2002). 'A Defence of the Four-Category Ontology', in *Argument und Analyse*, ed. C. U. Moulines and K. G. Niebergall. Paderborn: Mentis-Verlag: 225–40.
—— (2005). *The Four-Category Ontology*. Oxford: Oxford University Press.
Mackie, J. L. (1976). *Problems from Locke*. Oxford: Clarendon Press.
Mellor, D. H. (1977). 'Natural Kinds', in *Matters of Metaphysics*. Cambridge: Cambridge University Press: 123–35.
Molnar, G. (2003). *Powers*, ed. S. Mumford. Oxford: Oxford University Press.
Mumford, S. (1998). *Dispositions*. Oxford: Oxford University Press.
—— (2004). *Laws in Nature*. London: Routledge.
—— (2006). 'Powers, Dispositions, Properties', in *Revitalizing Causality*, ed. R. Groff. London: Routledge.
Putnam, H. (1975). 'The Meaning of "Meaning"', in *Mind, Language, and Reality*. Cambridge: Cambridge University Press: 215–71.
Quine, W. V. O. (1969). 'Natural Kinds', in *Ontological Relativity and Other Essays*. New York: Colombia University Press: 114–38.
Salmon, N. (1982). *Reference and Essence*. Oxford: Blackwell.
Shoemaker, S. (1984). 'Causality and Properties', in *Identity, Cause, and Mind*. Cambridge: Cambridge University Press: 206–33.
Wilkerson, T. (1995). *Natural Kinds*. Aldershot: Ashgate.

[11] Earlier versions of this paper were presented at the RIP symposium on natural kinds held at the University of Durham, the Institut Jean Nicod in Paris and the 2004 Ratio conference in Reading. I thank all who contributed to the subsequent discussions and those who have given me helpful comments outside these forums.

CHAPTER 5

LAWS AND ESSENCES

Alexander Bird

1. Dispositional essentialism

Many subjunctive conditionals are true; 'were I to place this salt in water, it would dissolve' is one I know to be so. What makes such conditionals true is often the existence of a dispositional property. On the simple conditional view of the concept of a disposition, that link is analytic. (For example: *x* is soluble in water *iff* were *x* placed in water, *x* would dissolve.) But there are reasons to think that the simple conditional analysis is false – the disposition might be finkish,[1] there may be antidotes present,[2] more generally conditions may not be ideal.[3] But even so, as Charlie Martin, who rejects the conditional analysis, admits, there is some connection between dispositions and conditionals.[4] What exactly the relation between disposition and conditional is has been widely discussed elsewhere. Mumford's 'conditional conditional' account, for example, claims that the relation is such that the disposition suffices for the truth of the conditional under ideal conditions (1998: 87–91). Dispositions can still be a crucial part of what makes conditionals true, even if their existence is not sufficient for that truth.[5] Let us now add the contentious claim that the connection between a particular dispositional property and the corresponding conditional is one that is essential to that property. This claim is contentious because a widespread view is that all natural properties are essentially categorical. The view I shall promote here is:

> (DE) Some properties are essentially dispositional and these properties include the properties that figure in the fundamental laws of nature.

---

[1] Martin (1994).
[2] Bird (1998).
[3] Mumford (1998).
[4] Armstrong, Martin and Place (1996: 178).
[5] For an extended discussion see Mellor (2000: 758–65).

When I say 'property' here, I mean what David Lewis signifies by 'sparse' property, that is a natural property, one which thus would be mentioned in some ideal complete science. (DE) says that at least all the fundamental sparse properties are essentially dispositional. (DE) leaves it open that all properties are essentially dispositional, but prima facie this is implausible: 'being made of clay', or 'being hydrogen' seem to be respectable properties but are not obviously dispositional. We might be able to conceive of such properties, properties of constitution, as being identical with complexes of dispositions: to be hydrogen is just to have all the dispositions that hydrogen has. But that is an issue to be addressed in full elsewhere.

(DE), the claim that fundamental sparse properties are essentially linked with characteristic subjunctive conditionals, is consistent with a denial that the instantiation of the disposition in question necessitates the truth of the corresponding conditional. What it does require is that the kind of ability that a disposition (strictly, its instantiation) has to make a conditional true in this world (when it is true) is repeated with respect to the same conditional in all other possible worlds. In another possible world the disposition might not in fact make the conditional true, but that will be because extrinsic conditions are not suitable; it will not be because in that world the disposition is irrelevant to that conditional. (Here I am talking about conditional-*types*, where the same conditional type (e.g. were x placed in y, x would dissolve) may be instantiated by different sets of individuals. The condition stated in the antecedent of such conditionals is the *stimulus* and in the consequent is the *manifestation*. I symbolise this subjunctive or counterfactual conditional thus: x is placed in y $\Box\!\!\rightarrow$ x dissolves.)

This view, dispositional essentialism, contrasts with a number of traditional and more modern views about the nature of properties and laws, and their roles in explaining the truth of conditionals.[6,7] Categoricalism I regard as the view:

(C) All properties are categorical.

---

[6] Dispositional essentialism is a view first promoted in Ellis and Lierse (1994). They do not define dispositional essentialism as I have done, but it is clear nonetheless that something like weak dispositional essentialism is close to the core of their position. Ellis has since expanded on his view in Ellis (2001, 2002).

[7] It is a solecism to confuse laws and law-statements. It is one that for the sake of convenience I shall consciously commit in what follows.

Understanding the term 'categorical' can be subject to misleading connotations. One such invites the following thought. An essentially dispositional property is only sometimes there, viz. only when it is being manifested in response to the appropriate stimulus; that is, the property's instantiation is conditional on that stimulus. By contrast, a categorical property is always there, not conditionally on anything. This is a mistake. Dispositions exist and are really there whether or not they are manifesting – the fragile vase is fragile even when not being struck and being broken. The fact that the manifestation is conditional on the stimulus does not make the disposition itself conditional on the stimulus. Nor should we see categorical properties as permanently manifesting properties – manifesting their own existence. First, a genuine disposition might permanently manifest itself, perhaps even necessarily so, without that making it categorical. Secondly, a manifestation is distinct from the property itself. To say that a property manifests itself in its own existence is to state a truism that holds of every property, dispositional or categorical.

What we mean by 'categorical' must be understood in negative terms. That is, a categorical property does not confer of necessity any power or disposition. Its existence does not, essentially, require it to manifest itself in any distinctive fashion in response to an appropriate stimulus. To say that a property is categorical is to deny that it is essentially dispositional. (C) implies the negation of (DE).

While, according to (C), the dispositional character of a property is in no case essential to that property, it is undeniable that there are properties with a dispositional character. The categoricalist regards that character as being imposed upon a property by the laws of nature. More generally the categoricalist holds:

(CL) The laws are metaphysically contingent relations among categorical properties.

Whether (CL) is entailed by (C) is unclear. One could hold that the laws of nature are metaphysically necessary, which would give categorical properties a necessary dispositional character. But this need not be equivalent to (DE) since something may have some feature necessarily without that feature being essential. However, that would leave unanswered the question of the source of the relevant metaphysical necessity – why should laws be necessary on this view?

As a matter of fact, no-one has taken this view and all those who hold (C) also hold (CL), and consequently I shall take it that categoricalism involves commitment to (CL). On a regularity view of laws, for example, a law is some sort of regularity among the instantiations of properties: all instances of the property F are instances of the property G $(\forall x(Fx{\rightarrow}Gx))$, or in a slightly more complex case, whenever both property S and property D are instantiated, then property M is instantiated $(\forall x((Dx\&Sx){\rightarrow}Mx))$.[8] If these are laws on the regularity view, then (according to the regularity theorist) we have explanations for the truth of subjunctive conditionals. The first law makes it true that were **a** F, then **a** would be G; the second makes it true that given that **b** is D, were **b** S, then **b** would be M. The latter also allows us to say (to a first approximation) what a disposition is, according to a regularity theorist. It is a property (such as D in the last example) that occurs in the antecedent of a law in conjunction with some other property (S), the stimulus property, where the consequent (M) in the law is the manifestation property. Regularity theorists hold that the regularities in question might not have held; in other possible worlds they do not. Hence in some other possible world, $\forall x((Dx\&Sx){\rightarrow}Mx)$ need not be true. In such a world, it might be the case that, for example, $\forall x((Dx\&Gx){\rightarrow}Fx)$. While in the actual world the property D bears a special relation to the conditional $(Sx\ \Box{\rightarrow}\ Mx)$, in this other world it bears that relation not to this conditional but to a different one, $(Gx\ \Box{\rightarrow}\ Fx)$. Since the same property may in different worlds be associated with different conditionals, the relation it actually has with some conditional and hence the dispositional character it actually has are contingent. Thus regularity theorists deny dispositional essentialism.

This denial is not exclusive to regularity theorists. It is made also by their opponents, the nomic necessitarians. For David Armstrong, laws are better understood as second-order relations of nomic necessitation among universals.[9] So the laws are not $\forall x(Fx{\rightarrow}Gx)$ and $\forall x((Dx\&Sx){\rightarrow}Mx)$, but are N(F, G) and N((D&S), M). But Armstrong does agree with the regularity theorist that these laws are contingent. In his metaphysics the

---

[8] A sophisticated regularity theorist will not regard every such regularity as a law. Additional conditions, such as being a consequence of a system of regularities that optimises simplicity and strength, will be required. Cf. Lewis (1973: 72–7).

[9] Armstrong (1983). See also Dretske (1977) and Tooley (1977).

relation of nomic necessitation, its name notwithstanding, might hold between certain universals in this world but not between those universals in another possible world. Thus Armstrong's understanding of dispositions is that they are properties such as D where in the world in question there is a law $N((D\&S), M)$.[10] Thus in the actual world D may be associated with the conditional 'were x to be S it would become M', but because the relation of necessitation may not hold in some other world, D will not be associated with that conditional in all worlds.

Clearly there is a deep difference between the dispositional essentialist on the one hand and both the regularity theorist and the nomic necessitarian on the other, about both the nature of laws and the nature of properties. Note that so far the dispositional essentialist has said nothing about the nature of laws. Where the anti-essentialists explain a subjunctive conditional by citing a property plus a contingent law, the essentialist cited only the property. It looks as if laws are otiose for the essentialist.[11] But it is better to regard them as simply supervening on the dispositional properties. Let us imagine that a simple essentialism were true, whereby the existence of the dispositional property entails the corresponding conditional, i.e. Dx entails $Sx \mathbin{\Box\!\!\rightarrow} Mx$. Let it be the case that for some $\mathbf{a}$, $D\mathbf{a}$. Because of this entailment, $(S\mathbf{a} \mathbin{\Box\!\!\rightarrow} M\mathbf{a})$. And now let it be that $S\mathbf{a}$; hence we have $M\mathbf{a}$. Thus it is true that $((D\mathbf{a}\&S\mathbf{a})\rightarrow M\mathbf{a})$; and generalizing gives us $\forall x((Dx\&Sx)\rightarrow Mx)$. So merely the existence of the property D generates what the regularity theorist takes to be a law. If we allow ourselves to think in terms of universals, then we may take the conditional-type to be really a relation among universals, 'S $\mathbin{\Box\!\!\rightarrow}$ M'. Since this relation holds by virtue of the existence of the universal D, we have that D&S 'necessitates' M (by parallel reasoning to the foregoing). By necessitates here, I mean the following: universal F necessitates universal G, when for any particular x, Fx entails Gx. We need only interpret 'necessitates' as being identical to or entailing Armstrong's 'N', to have Armstrong's law. Thus the dispositional essentialist view can be seen as generating what the regularity theorists and nomic necessitarians take to be laws. (Note that we have taken the simple case where Dx entails $Sx \mathbin{\Box\!\!\rightarrow} Mx$. As I will shortly mention, where this is not strictly true we will have a *ceteris paribus* law.)

---

[10] Armstrong (1997: 80–3).
[11] Mumford (2004) takes an eliminativist view of laws on roughly these grounds.

That is not to say that advocates of contingent necessitation or of the regularity view should be happy with dispositional essentialism. The sophisticated regularity theorist will have constraints upon laws that the essentialist's view will not meet, such as the need for the law to figure in some optimal systematization of regularities. More significant for current concerns is the fact that the essentialist view makes the laws of nature necessary. In deriving the laws I assumed only the existence of the property D. Hence in any possible world in which D exists, the corresponding law exists too. And so, according to the dispositional essentialist, it is not true that there might be a world in which things are D but where there is no law (strict or *ceteris paribus*) relating D, S, and M.

The above shows that (DE) has the following consequence, partial necessitarianism about laws:

(PNL) At least some of the laws of nature are metaphysically necessary.

An ambitious dispositional essentialist may wish to go beyond partial necessitarianism to full necessitarianism:

(FNL) All the laws of nature are metaphysically necessary.

The fact that (DE) can explain some of the laws of nature inspires the thought that it might explain them all. Accepting (PNL) but not (FNL) would give us a mixed view of laws, some explained as consequences of (DE) while others are explained à la façon de Lewis or à la façon d'Armstrong. This would seems to be an untidy metaphysic, with two classes of laws. Theorists have always sought a unified account of laws. If we accept:

(U) Whatever it is, the true account of fundamental laws is a unified account

then a commitment to (PNL) becomes a commitment to (FNL).

As I have mentioned above, simple essentialism is not generally true – although it might be true of some specific properties. I said that a property might be essentially linked with a conditional without entailing it. But if the existence of the property does not entail the conditional, it looks as if it will not entail the corresponding law either. Rather than being an objection to the dispositional essentialist account of laws, this provides the opportunity to explain non-strict laws. A property that does not entail the related conditional may nonetheless generate not a strict law but a *ceteris paribus* law. The manifestation of charge is that like charges repel and unlike attract. So it will be a (necessary) law that like charges repel. But this is a *ceteris paribus* law, for if the charged bodies have sufficient mass then the gravitational attraction will exceed the electrostatic repulsion and they will attract not repel.[12] The conditions corresponding to finks and, especially, antidotes will be those that are the *ceteris paribus* conditions in the corresponding law. Thus dispositional essentialism gives a natural account not only of strict but also of *ceteris paribus* laws.[13]

2. Quidditism

In part 1 above I sketched the view of laws that flows from taking properties to be essentially dispositional – a view which is articulated first by Chris Swoyer (1982) and later by Brian Ellis and Caroline Lierse (1994) and which draws on a conception of properties closely related to that advocated by Sydney Shoemaker (1984). I shall now argue that this dispositionalist view of properties has advantages over the categoricalist view.

In part 1, I adverted to the fact that for both regularity theorists of law and nomic necessitarians, the nomic features of a universal are contingent. In other possible worlds they might be connected in other laws with universals with which they have no connection in this world. Hence the dispositional character, the causal powers and other such properties of universals are not essential to them. As David Lewis says, 'there isn't much to the intrinsic nature of a universal' (1986: 205) and as Robert Black describes Lewis's view of qualities (properties, universals),

> Lewis follows Hume in denying that fundamental properties have, let alone consist of, essential causal powers. . . . Just about all there is to a Humean fundamental quality is its identity with itself and its distinctness from other qualities. A Humean fundamental quality is intrinsically inert and self-contained (2000: 91).

[12] This is an account of fundamental laws and one need not expect that all laws will have the form, when expressed as generalizations, $\forall x((Dx \& Sx) \to Mx)$. Laws supervening on such laws need not have such a form. The law that protons repel positrons will be a consequence of the *ceteris paribus* law considered plus the essences of protons and positrons (which in each case involves their being positively charged).

[13] But see Drewery (2001) for the view that laws cannot be reduced to dispositional properties of individuals, as opposed to dispositions of kinds.

If we allow one and the same universal to appear in distinct possible worlds, then, as Black notes, this Humean view of universals is akin to haecceitism about particulars. I shall regard the core of haecceitism to be the view that the transworld identity of particulars does not supervene on their qualitative features.[14] Black calls haecceitism about universals 'quidditism', which he takes to be 'the acceptance of primitive identity between fundamental qualities across possible worlds.' By 'primitive' we mean an identity that is not dependent on identity of causal roles or powers more generally. (Henceforth I shall refer to the causal powers and dispositional features associated with a property as its 'powers'.[15] Roughly, the powers of a property are the dispositions conferred on an object by possessing that property.) Although Black discusses quidditism with regard to Lewis's metaphysics, we should note that Armstrong is equally committed to quidditism. Whatever powers a property has it has contingently as a consequence of the contingent laws in which it is involved. There is equally little to the essential nature of a property on Armstrong's view as there is on Lewis's.

It is useful to distinguish here various elements to quidditism. First, says Black, according to the quidditist, fundamental properties do not have essential powers. I shall liberalise this to say that such properties do not have any powers of necessity.

(QA1) For all fundamental universals F and powers X there is a world where F lacks X.

Now let us consider a world w_1 where F does have X. (QA1) tells us that there is some world where F lacks X. Because we are dealing with fundamental universals, we can say that the nearest possible world where F lacks X is one which is, in fundamental respects, just like w_1, except in just that F lacks X. (If we were dealing with differences at a non-fundamental level, then we could not say this.) For example, in Lewis's view the nearest such world will be one where the regularity which relates F, the stimu-

---

[14] Where 'qualitative features' are taken to exclude properties of identity.

[15] I do not call them *causal* powers for two reasons. First, I do not want to give the impression that the notion 'causal power' is to be analysed in terms of causation. If anything the relationship is the reverse. Secondly, it may turn out that causation is only a macro-level phenomenon, but that powers exist at the fundamental level. An additional point: it is implicit in this that there are no causal or other powers independent of laws/dispositions. While singularists about causation might think that a particular has its causal powers independently of law, it is difficult to see how a universal could have or confer causal powers without generating what we would naturally think of as a law.

lus property of the power S, and the manifestation property M, will not hold – there will be one exception. In Armstrong's view F will not be related by contingent nomic necessitation, N, to S and M. These changes can be made leaving all other fundamental features of the world intact.

(QA2) For any world w_1, any fundamental universal F, and any power X, where at w_1, universal F has X, there is a world w_2 like w_1 in all fundamental respects except that the very same universal F lacks X.

If a universal can lose a power with ease, it can also gain one. Categorical properties are all essentially alike – differing only in their mutual distinctness. So if one categorical property can have a certain power, so can another, in some world. Given that in w_1 F lacks X, what is the nearest world in which F possesses X? It will be just like w_1, except that (i) F possesses X and (ii) F loses any powers possessed in w_1 that are incompatible with F's possessing X. Thus:

(QA3) For any world w_1, any fundamental universal F, and any power X, where at w_1, universal F lacks X, there is a world w_2 like w_1 in all fundamental respects except (i) that very same universal F possesses X, and (ii) F does not possess any powers inconsistent with X.

(DE) states that fundamental universals do have essential powers, and hence (DE) $\Rightarrow \neg$(QA1) (and (DE) $\Rightarrow \neg$(QA2) and (DE) $\Rightarrow \neg$(QA3)). Since both (DE) and (QA1) are claims about *all* fundamental properties, the denials of both are consistent with one another – if one denies both one holds that some fundamental properties have dispositional essences and others do not. However, if, as I suggested for laws, we adopt as an assumption of the debate that we should give a unified account of the metaphysics of fundamental properties (one that ascribes the same modal character to all – either all have dispositional essences or none have) then (DE) $\Leftrightarrow \neg$(QA1).

Secondly, we may adopt the analogue of the core of haecceitism as I defined it above: the transworld identity of universals does not supervene on their qualitative properties, where now 'qualitative properties' means powers.

(QB1) Two distinct worlds, w_3 and w_4 may be alike in all respects except that: (i) at w_3, universal F has powers

$\{C_1, C_2, \ldots\}$; (ii) at w_4, universal G has powers $\{C_1, C_2, \ldots\}$; (iii) F ≠ G.

(QB1) captures the idea that sameness of powers does not entail identity of universal. Strictly this is consistent with dispositional essentialism. The fact that one property has its powers necessarily is consistent with some distinct property having those same powers (also necessarily). However, just as essentialism aims to give an account of what laws are, it may also aim to account for the nature of, at least, fundamental properties. That is, not only are the powers of a property essential to that property, they are the essence of the property – they constitute what it is to be that property. Thus identity of powers entails identity of property. This view I shall call strong dispositional essentialism (SDE). The difference between (henceforth weak) essentialism and strong essentialism is captured in Black's statement of what Lewis and Hume deny, 'that fundamental properties have, let alone consist of, essential powers'. The denial of *having* essential powers is the denial of weak essentialism, and the denial of *consisting of* essential powers is the denial of strong essentialism. Thus (SDE) = (DE) + ¬(QB1) Strong essentialism makes the identity of fundamental properties require identity of powers. The further claim that strong essentialism makes over weak essentialism is pretty well what Shoemaker famously argues for in 'Causality and Properties' where he says,

> what makes a property the property it is, what determines its identity, is its potential for contributing to the powers of things that have it. . . . if under all possible circumstances properties X and Y make the same contribution to the powers of the things that have them, X and Y are the same property (1984: 212).

In this discussion I have been careful to distinguish (QA1) and (QB1). However, as we shall see, (QA1) in fact entails (QB1), via (QA2) and (QA3). (Note, nonetheless, that because the negation of (QA1) does not entail the negation of (QB1), weak and strong essentialism are still distinct.)

Against quidditism – (QA1)

Haecceitism about individuals is discussed, and rejected, by Roderick Chisholm (1967). Chisholm considers changes to the properties of two individuals, Adam and Noah, in a sequence of possible worlds, so that at each change from one world to the next we are, it is supposed, happy to say that the change in properties does not change the identities of the individuals. We then find that in the final world Adam has all the properties Noah has in the actual world, and vice versa (including the names people call them). The transitivity of identity requires that the final world is distinct from the actual world. But Chisholm takes it to be absurd that there should be a world like this that is not the actual world. If he is right, then haecceitism is false. He draws a disjunctive conclusion, that either there are essential properties (we were wrong to assume that every change of property across worlds leaves identity intact), or transworld identity of particulars is misconceived. Since he has what he takes to be reasons for thinking that essential properties are absurd, he adopts the second disjunct. This is of course Lewis's view about particulars, which each exist only in one world but may have counterparts in others. Interestingly Lewis does not reject transworld identity for universals – and the force of Black's argument against Lewis is that Lewis cannot both be a genuine (or concrete as opposed to ersatz or mathematical) modal realist while remaining a quidditist, someone who allows for transworld identity of Humean properties. Black raises counterparts for properties as one option for Lewis (not Black's preferred option). However, this is not the only option, even for genuine modal realists. It is my view that Chisholm should have accepted that individuals have essential properties. I shall argue that we should accept that analogous view of properties, that they have essential powers.

It may be noted that Chisholm's argument is not against the core of haecceitism as I defined it – that the transworld identity of particulars does not supervene on their qualitative features. Rather it is against the following:

(H0) Two distinct worlds, w_1 and w_2 may be alike in all respects except that: (i) at w_1, particular **a** has qualities F_1, F_2, F_3 ... and a distinct particular **b** has qualities G_1, G_2, G_3 ... ;

(ii) at w_2, the particular **a** has qualities G_1, G_2, G_3 ... and particular **b** has qualities F_1, F_2, F_3 ... ;

(iii) $\forall i \, \forall j \, (F_i \neq G_j)$

(H0) is a substantial claim. The simplest expression of haecceitism is that particulars lack essential properties. In what follows, 'properties' are limited to intrinsic properties that not all particulars have of necessity (i.e. not self-identity, not the property such that $2 + 2 = 4$, etc.). Thus:

(H1) For any particular **a** and any property F there is a world where **a** lacks F.

which corresponds to (QA1). Just as (QA1) leads to (QA2) and (QA3), (H1) leads to:

(H2) For any world w_1, any particular **a**, and any property F, where at w_1, **a** has F there is a world w_2 like w_1 in all respects except that **a** lacks X.

(H3) For any world w_1, any particular **a**, and any property F, where at w_1, **a** lacks F, there is a world w_2 like w_1 in all respects except (i) that **a** is F, and (ii) **a** does not possess any properties inconsistent with X.

Put less formally, the haecceitist conception of particulars is that they are essentially all alike, differing only in that they are mutually distinct. Identity is independent of qualities in a very strong sense. Any property a particular has it could lack and any it does not have it could possess; in general any particular may possess or lack any consistent set of qualities. Is Chisholm correct in ascribing (H0) to the haecceitist? I think he is. Since all particulars are essentially alike, it is possible for one to possess all the properties of another and vice versa. Furthermore, Chisholm provides a story about how we get to (H0) via repeated applications of (H2) and (H3). Neighbouring worlds differ only as regards the lack/possession of a single quality.

As mentioned, (H2) and (H3) are the haecceitist analogues of the quidditist (QA2) and (QA3). Correspondingly, quidditism is committed to the truth of:

(QA0) Two distinct worlds, w_1 and w_2 may be alike in all respects except that: (i) at w_1, universal F has powers X_1, X_2, X_3 ... and a distinct universal G has powers Y_1, Y_2, Y_3 ... ; (ii) at w_2, the universal F has powers Y_1, Y_2, Y_3 ... and universal G has powers X_1, X_2, X_3 ... ; (iii) $\forall i \; \forall j \; (X_i \neq X_j)$

This seems right. If, as Black says, the quidditist conception of properties is that they have primitive identity, identity that is completely independent of their powers, then there should be no reason why we cannot swap powers without swapping universals – or swap universals without swapping powers.

Now consider the following descriptions of worlds:

w_a The actual world (assuming a Newtonian account of the laws of nature).

w_b Like w_a except there is no negative charge.

w_c Like w_b except that:
(i) inertial mass is not proportional to gravitational mass;
(ii) inertial mass is proportional to charge.

w_d Like w_c except that there is negative gravitational mass (Newton's laws of gravitation still holds, so a negative mass and a positive mass repel).

w_e Like w_d except that the signs in Newton's law of gravitation and Coulomb's law are both changed. (Thus two positive charges attract; two positive gravitational masses repel; a positive and a negative gravitational mass attract.)

w_e is a world where charge has all the causal or nomic roles associated with gravitational mass, including proportionality with inertial mass, while gravitational mass has the causal/nomic roles of charge. We can also describe a world w_f like the actual world except that the roles of gravitational mass and inertial mass have been swapped. Consequently we can also describe a world w_g like the actual world except that the roles of charge and inertial mass have been swapped.

The worlds w_e, w_f, and w_g are analogues for properties of Chisholm's final world with every property of Adam and Noah swapped. Just as Chisholm wants to say about Noah and Adam, if anything exists which seems to fit our description of w_e, then it is just the actual world plus a decision to swap the names 'gravitational mass' and 'charge'; similarly if anything exists which seems to fit our description of w_g, then it is just the actual world plus a decision to swap the names 'inertial mass' and 'charge'. Indeed, I think our intuitions tell us that there is something wrong about worlds w_b to w_d as well.

Just as we should reject haecceitism we should reject quidditism, which we may do by allowing both particulars and properties to have essential properties. Chisholm does not go down this road for particulars, for two reasons. First, he thinks that we would have no way of knowing what the essential properties are. Secondly, he thinks that the essentialist would be committed to the view that knowing, for example, who the bank robber is would require knowing of some x, whose essential properties are E, that x has E and x robbed the bank. But neither of these are good grounds for doubting essentialism. To the first one may make two replies. First, if we are to believe Kripke, we do know what an individual person's essential properties are (or at least include), and that is a matter of coming from some particular egg and sperm. Secondly, whether or not Kripke is right, our ignorance of which the essential properties are is not itself a strong reason for doubting the coherence of the view that says that they exist. Turning to the second problem, the issue of essential properties, in this context, is a matter of transworld identity. Presumably the detective is interested in capturing the criminal in this world, not in tracking him down in some other world. Therefore knowledge of *contingent* properties that enable the detective to pick the robber out from other *actual* people is all that is required.

Essentialism thus seems a good bet for delivering us from haecceitism about individuals. And it is equally serviceable for avoiding quidditism about properties. If inertial mass, charge and so forth are qualities that confer the powers that they do necessarily, then the descriptions of worlds w_b to w_g do not describe genuine possibilities. The Chisholmian intuitions that lead us to reject those putative possible worlds can only encourage us to reject strong quidditism.

Against quidditism – (QB1)

Assuming a uniform metaphysics of properties, rejecting (QA1) is the same as accepting weak essentialism. But weak essentialism is compatible with (QB1). (QB1) allows that the essential properties of a property may not be enough to establish its identity – two properties may have the same essential powers.

What then might inspire us to make the transition to strong essentialism from weak essentialism? Equivalently, what reason is there to adopt the Shoemaker line about properties, that their powers establish their identity?

Consider:

> (QB2) One and the same world w is such that: (i) at w, universal F has powers $\{C_1, C_2, \ldots\}$; (ii) at w, universal G has powers $\{C_1, C_2, \ldots\}$; (iii) F $\neq$ G.

(QB2) differs from (QB1) in that whereas (QB1) contemplates distinct worlds where distinct properties have the same powers, (QB2) allows a single world to contain distinct properties with the same powers. Despite this difference, I believe that (QB2) is implied by the quidditist picture. If identity is independent of powers, why shouldn't two properties possess the same powers in the same world? Furthermore, it looks as if we can get to (QB2) by iterated applications of (QB1), in a manner similar to Chisholm's strategy. In Chisholm's original story, we considered swapping the qualities of Adam and Noah one by one. But if instead we considered just half this story, the changes that happen to Noah, so gradually Noah loses his own properties and acquires Adam's, without Adam undergoing any change, then we will end up with two particulars, Adam and Noah, in the same world with identical qualities. The same strategy applied to properties gives us (QB2). (QA1), thanks to its implications in (QA2) and (QA3), allows the loss and gain of powers quite without consideration of whether those powers are possessed by any other property. *A fortiori* (QA1) permits us to start with a world where F has powers $\{C_1, C_2, \ldots\}$ whereas G does not, and for G to lose and gain powers until we end up with a world where G has powers $\{C_1, C_2, \ldots\}$ without considering the existence of a distinct F with those same powers. The same argument shows how (QA1) yields worlds as described by (QB1).

(QB2) envisages two properties entering into entirely parallel causal roles and nomic relations. I.e., let F and G be properties, and let it be the case that for every other property H, it is a law that Fs are Hs iff it is a law that Gs are Hs, and so on. If this were the case, then F and G would be indistinguishable – where there seemed to be one law there would in fact be two. Applied to the case of inertial mass, the idea is that there might be two fundamental properties that are actually responsible for its being such that if a force is applied then a corresponding acceleration would result, mass$_A$ and mass$_B$. If something accelerates with acceleration a when subjected to force F, there would be two potential explanations for this, that the entity has mass$_A$ equal in magnitude to F/a or that it has mass$_B$ equal to that magnitude. If weak quidditism were correct we would not know whether we are in such a world or not, or indeed in such a world there are many, many parallel properties, each of which is possessed by exactly one bearer.

The foregoing consequence of (QB2), adverted to by Shoemaker (1984: 215), does serious damage to our concept of property. Nonetheless, at first sight, categoricalists might be able to bite this bullet. But they should contemplate a more obviously troubling difficulty thereby created for our understanding of dispositional and theoretical terms. For example, Prior (1985: 64) suggests two ways a categoricalist might understand 'inertial mass': inertial mass = the property responsible for being such that if a force were applied then a finite acceleration would result; or, inertial mass = the property *actually* responsible for being such that if a force were applied then a finite acceleration would result. The first proposal is that 'inertial mass' stands for a definite description, while on the second 'inertial mass' is a rigid designator that picks out at a possible world precisely that property that in the *actual* world has the relevant kinematic effects. As far as I can tell, Armstrong regards the second or something like it as the appropriate understanding. Now consider a world as described where two distinct properties both do the same causal work of responding to a force with an acceleration. Then the term 'inertial mass' would fail to refer, on both glosses.

Similarly, Lewis (1970) explicates theoretical terms by elaborating on the idea of a Ramsey sentence. The Ramsey sentence of a theory $T(t_1, t_2, t_3, \ldots, t_n)$, which contains the theoretical terms $t_1, t_2, t_3, \ldots, t_n$, is the sentence $\exists x_1, \exists x_2, \exists x_3, \ldots \exists x_n \ T(x_1, x_2, x_3, \ldots x_n)$. Lewis's idea is that we regard the terms $t_1, t_2, t_3, \ldots, t_n$ as referring only if the open sentence $T(x_1, x_2, x_3, \ldots x_n)$ is uniquely satisfied. If the latter is the case then the term t_i refers to the entity e_i in the unique n-tuple $<e_1, e_2, e_3 \ldots e_n>$ that satisfies $T(x_1, x_2, x_3, \ldots x_n)$. In a world where there are parallel properties, both of which stand in the relation T to other properties, there will be failure of reference of the corresponding theoretical terms. The possibility of failure of reference of theoretical terms is not itself a problem – we know this possibility to be actualized in some cases. What is worrying is the thought that we can never know that the possibility is not actualized for any theoretical term – we never know whether any such term refers.

It appears that Lewis later changed his mind to regard cases of multiple realisation as involving indeterminate reference.[16] I am not sure what indeterminate reference is. The law of the excluded middle requires that either t refers to e or t does not refer to e. In any case we are still left in the position of never knowing whether our theoretical terms (determinately) refer. Lewis says that the original injunction to regard reference as failing in the case of multiple realisation was supposed to meet the intention of the

16   Lewis, 'Ramseyan Humility'.

theorist to give an implicit definition of his terms. That may be the intention of the theorist. What is clearer is that the theorist intended to refer (determinately). For if the theorist had intended to leave open the possibility of multiple realisation, the theorist would not have used a theoretical term (a referring expression) but instead would have used quantifiers (as in the Ramsey sentence). Put another way, the proper Ramsey sentence for $T(t)$ is not $\exists x T(x)$ at all but rather $\exists! x T(x)$. Lewis seems to concur, saying that we should write the postulate in such a way that the theory cannot be multiply realised. If we do that, we have no way of knowing whether our theory is true or not, since we have no way of knowing that it is not multiply realised by functionally parallel but categorically distinct properties. Lewis accepts and indeed argues for the thesis that quidditism entails Humility, where Humility is the claim that we cannot know about the fundamental properties of nature. Lewis may have been content to accept both quidditism and Humility. But *this* sceptical consequence of Humility is, I suggest, a very high price to pay for the Humean metaphysic.

We do not want our metaphysics of properties to condemn us to necessary ignorance of them. And so we should reject quidditism. Since categoricalism entails quidditism (strong and weak), we should reject categoricalism too. The problems concerning identity and reference raised by quidditism are immediately resolved by adopting strong dispositional essentialism, the view that the identity of properties is fixed by their essential powers.

3. Structural properties

In this section I will consider the objection to (DE) raised by Brian Ellis (2006). This concerns geometrical, numerical, spatial, temporal properties, and other properties that I call 'structural'. The concern is that while other properties have dispositional essences, it is difficult to see that these ones do. On the other hand we cannot just ignore such properties, for they do play a part in scientific explanations. A cylinder can be made to roll down an inclined plane of less than 45 degrees but a triangular or square prism cannot. It is the shape of the cross-sections that explains such facts. The law of gravitation tells us how gravitational force depends on spatial separation. And so on. If the fundamental properties of science include such properties then, it seems, some fundamental properties are categorical.[17]

I will first consider whether the problem raised in part 2 against categorical properties can somehow be avoided for these properties. Here is a suggestion. The problem arises for property terms which are introduced by a description of their theoretical role. But not all properties need be introduced that way. For example, we can understand 'triangle' via a definition ('plane figure with three straight edges'). Or we can understand the same term via direct ostension of triangles. Similarly we can fix a standard of spatial displacement (distance) with a sample (a ruler or standard measure). These might be direct ways of relating to categorical properties, as contrasted with the indirect route via a role in a scientific theory or explanation.

This perspective is, however, misleading, for various reasons. First, the claims of dispositional essentialism are intended to apply only to fundamental properties. And there is no reason to suppose that properties identified in the manners described will be ones that appear in fundamental science (the ostensive definition of spatial and temporal quantities may appear to be an exception – I shall return to these). In particular we should not expect composite properties, those defined in terms of a composition of parts (such as triangle) to figure in fundamental science. Secondly, we have no guarantee that the methods under discussion (ostension and definition) will pick out genuine natural properties, fundamental or not. Let us consider a parallel case, the ostension of natural kinds of substance. We may be able to define a natural kind term (e.g., 'gold') by ostension. But *a posteriori* investigation is required to establish that we have successfully done so. If the ostended sample is not a single substance but a mixture, then we will not have defined a kind term. Furthermore, the distinction between mixtures and compounds, which is required to ground the ostension of many chemical natural kinds, is itself a product of chemical theory. Thus ostension cannot bypass theory in the definition of kind terms. Nor can it do so for property terms. One might have thought, nonetheless, that if there *is* a single kind being ostended, then one has succeeded in picking out that kind rather than some functionally parallel kind.

---

[17] A similar point is made by Molnar (2003: 158–62).

However, it is not merely a simplification to think of ostensive definition as being a single event. There is no single sample of gold that fixes the extension of the term 'gold'. We multiply and repeatedly characterise that extension via acts of ostension. Our ability to do so depends on its being the case that most of the samples are indeed instances of the same substance. That can be confirmed by empirical investigation, and again that will depend on the employment of a relevant theory. In some cases we may find out that the samples are not all the same, as in the case of jade, and that we have not picked out a natural kind. In such cases we can find out whether we have we have succeeded (or failed) in characterising a kind by investigation of the structure and composition of the samples. But in the case of fundamental properties that is just what we cannot do.

Let us turn to spatial and temporal properties. These might well seem to be quantities that we can define ostensively and which appear in fundamental physical theory but do not themselves have an essentially dispositional character. Again there is no guarantee that the macro-quantities are related to fundamental micro-quantities just by 'scaling-down'. The more we discover about space and time as revealed by basic physics, the less it resembles the three more-or-less Euclidean spatial dimensions and one temporal dimension that the macro-world appears to occupy. Indeed space-time might not be a fundamental entity at all and hence measures of space and time might not be fundamental either. (Compare the temperature of a gas, which is a macro-quantity that has no corresponding micro-quantity.) Nor can we assume, therefore, even if there are fundamental spatial and temporal quantities, that these are the same as the macro-quantities. Again, it is a matter of scientific discovery whether this is so. Consequently the terms that a fundamental theory would employ to name such quantities will be theoretical terms. Hence the problems raised for categorical properties will apply to these properties also. More generally, it is a mistake to think that we are acquainted with any natural property as it is, independently of its causal powers, since if we know about a property at all it is via its effect on its. As Marc Lange puts it,

> Geometric properties, like size and shape, may initially seem to be ideal cases of properties we know in themselves. But insofar as these are *physical* properties, to be instantiated by matter in space and not merely by abstract mathematical enti-

ties, it is not obvious that our senses disclose to us these properties as such (2002: 87).

Lange's remark may also help us see why it does not help that we
think we can grasp 'triangle' simply through its definition as a
'plane figure with three straight edges'. The possibility of abstract
definition does not show that we have defined a property such
that we can know, independently of any theory, that it is physically
possible for some object to possess it.

The next question is this: can structural properties be attributed with dispositional essences, contra Ellis? One way to show
that they can be would be to identify a subjunctive conditional
(perhaps with a *ceteris paribus* condition) entailed by an ascription
of a structural property. Hugh Mellor (1974) identifies such a conditional for the property of triangularity: x is triangular entails:
if x's corners were counted correctly, the result would be three.
This claim has been challenged by Elizabeth Prior (1985), not,
ultimately, successfully (in my opinion; see my 2003). But the
problem with this conditional is that it seems not to provide
the real essence of triangularity, since the disposition mentions
the human process of counting. But if structural properties
are to function in a fundamental science we do not want their
essences to be anthropocentric. Sungho Choi has suggested to me
that we could generalize the notion of counting corners. All we
would need is a counting machine that can distinguish travelling
along a geodesic from not doing so. If it did not do so at any point,
then it would add one. Such a machine, travelling along a triangular path, starting at any non-apex point, would count to three
on returning to its starting position. Even so, one might hope to
find an essence constituted out of properties that one might
expect to find in a fundamental theory. For example:

> <The paths AB, BC, and AC form a triangle> entails <if a signal
> S travels along AB then immediately along BC, and a signal S*
> travels along AC, starting at the same time and moving at the
> same speed, then S* will reach C before S>.

The problem with this is that it is false for many non-Euclidean
triangles. One possibility would be to regard 'triangle' as ambigu-
ous, or generic, across a range of triangle-properties, each for different kinds of geometry, and each of which has a different
essence of this kind.

However, we should remember that 'triangular' is unlikely itself
to be a fundamental structural property, and the dispositional

essentialist is thus not required to find a dispositional essence for it. It is the fundamental structural (primarily spatial and temporal) properties that have dispositional essences. Our knowledge of the nature of space and time is in a state of flux and we do not know what the role of fundamental spatial and temporal properties will be in the final theory of everything. Note that it is not *a priori* that such a theory would refer to spatial and temporal properties at all, nor, if it does, that the fundamental ones neatly mirror the role of such properties in folk physics or classical physics.

Nonetheless, we can make some prognostications that suggest that a final theory would treat all fundamental properties dispositionally. I will first mention a brief response by Stephen Mumford (2004: 188) to the current problem. The gravitational force on an object is sensitive to both the masses of it and other massy objects and its displacement from those other objects; looking at Newton's law: $F = Gm_1m_2/r^2$, the force F is a function of the masses m_1 and m_2 and also of their displacement r. That equation does not treat mass and displacement differently. In which case why should we not regard the force as a manifestation of the displacement, in which case displacement is characterised dispositionally (the displacement r between two points is the disposition whose manifestation, when masses m_1 and m_2 are located at the points, is a force between those masses with magnitude $F = Gm_1m_2/r^2$)?

While I think this is along the right lines, it needs supplementation. First, we need some explanation as to why it seems so much more natural to regard the force as a manifestation of the masses rather than of their displacement. Speaking figuratively we are inclined to think of the force as being generated by the masses, not by the displacement. Secondly, displacement crops up not just in the law of gravitation, but also in Coulomb's law and elsewhere. Thus it would appear that we could characterise displacement dispositionally with respect to a variety of different and seemingly independent manifestations. Should we think of displacement as a multi-track disposition (one with more than one kind of manifestation)? But that would be reason to suppose that displacement is not fundamental. Or is one of these manifestations (e.g. gravitational rather than electric force) privileged over the others?

The classical conception of space-time has been that of a stage or container within which things and laws act, but which is not itself involved in the action. It is a mere *background*. As such, although terms for spatial and temporal dimensions appear in the laws, we do not regard these terms as indicating action on the part of space and time. One manifestation of this is conventionalism about space-time, à la Mach, Poincaré, Schlick, or Duhem for example. According to views of this sort, a choice of geometry and metric is conventional. We typically choose our geometry in such a way as to make the laws of physics expressible in a convenient form. The choice does not reflect some fact concerning the real structure of space and time. If a spatial property, such as the distance between two points, is in effect the result of a conventional choice, rather than a real property of a real thing, then it is difficult to regard it as being active. Certainly this view would reject Mumford's claim that structural properties could be seen as dispositional properties with characteristic manifestations, on the same footing as the property of mass. A defender of (DE) (all fundamental, natural properties are essentially dispositional) may reply at this point that conventionalism is in effect arguing that spatial properties are not really natural properties at all, being simply the product of conventional choices. Hence the apparent exceptions do not fall under the scope of (DE) after all. At the same time, the awkward fact remains that spatial and temporal terms appear in our best scientific theories. One way of reading the debate between substantivalists and relativists regarding space and time is that the substantivalists, being impressed by the appearance of space and time in our laws, want to elevate space and time to something unarguably real, a substance, while the relativists noting that space and time are a mere background, not an agent, want to downplay space and time, holding them to be merely relative or conventional. In effect both camps recognize a deep tension between the presence of space and time in our laws and their role as a mere background – and both give an inadequate response, since neither fully eliminates a component of the tension.

Recently physicists such as John Baez (2001), Lee Smolin (1991), and Carlo Rovelli (1997) have advocated the view that a good physical theory should be background-free. Thus either space and time should be eliminated from our theories (although an unlikely prospect, this is not impossible). Or they should be shown not to be merely background. Either way the grounds for spatial and temporal properties and relations being exceptions to (DE) would be removed – in the first case because the properties no longer figure in fundamental science *at all*, and so are not fundamental, natural properties; and in the second case because space and time would no longer be background but fully fledged agents, capable of acting and being acted upon, and so permitting spatial and temporal properties to be understood dispositionally. General Relativity endorses the second alternative. Each space-time point is characterised by its dynamical properties, i.e. its disposition to affect the kinetic properties of an object at that point, captured in the gravitational field tensor at that point. The mass of each object is its disposition to change the curvature of space-time, that is to change the dynamical properties of each space-time point. Hence all the relevant explanatory properties in this set-up may be characterised dispositionally. And furthermore, this relationship explains why gravity is privileged over other forces in characterizing the essence of spatial relations.

4. Conclusion

In this paper I have examined in detail the prospects for explaining the nature of laws as reflecting the essences of the relevant natural properties. Those essences may be characterised dispositionally. Properties are what properties do. This contrasts with the view of, for example, Armstrong, according to which properties just are, and what they do depends on what the laws tell them to do – properties are categorical.

That properties are categorical and have no essential natures beyond being themselves involves a commitment to quidditism, a commitment shared by Lewis also. I argued that dispositional essentialism, unlike strong quidditism, does not lead to Chisholm's paradox for properties. And if we extend essentialism by making it an account of the nature and identity of at least fundamental properties, following Shoemaker, then we can also avoid the undisprovable possibility of a parallelism about properties that would make knowledge about the reference of theoretical terms impossible.

The latter problem is a problem for a quidditist/categoricalist conception of *any* property. Hence dispositional essentialism ought to apply to all properties. This invites the objection from Ellis and others, that structural properties, such as spatial relations, are rightly considered categorical. I argued that we are not obliged to see them as such. Since the thesis I am defending is one about the fundamental properties of physics, we cannot be sure that spatial properties are categorical until we understand the role of those properties in a true fundamental theory. I have proposed that our inclination to think that spatial properties are categorical is a reflection of the fact that we treat space and time as a background for our theories. But if we ought to make our theories background free, then we ought not allow ourselves to think in such a way that permits spatial properties to be categorical. And indeed General Relativity suggests that we should not.

References

Armstrong, D. M. (1983). *What is a Law of Nature?* Cambridge: Cambridge University Press.
—— (1997). *A World of States of Affairs.* Cambridge: Cambridge University Press.
Armstrong, D. M., Martin, C. B. and Place U. T. (1996). *Dispositions: A Debate*, ed. T. Crane. London: Routledge.
Baez, J. (2001). 'Higher Dimensional Algebra and Planck-Scale Physics', in *Physics Meets Philosophy at the Planck Scale*, ed. C. Callender and N. Huggett. Cambridge: Cambridge University Press.
Bird, A. (1998). 'Dispositions and Antidotes', *Philosophical Quarterly* 48.
—— (2003). 'Structural Properties', in *Real Metaphysics: Essays in Honour of D. H. Mellor*, ed. H. Lillehammer and G. Rodriguez-Pereyra: 154–168. London: Routledge.
Black, R. (2000). 'Against Quidditism', *Australasian Journal of Philosophy* 78: 87–104.
Chisholm, R. (1967). 'Identity through Possible Worlds: Some Questions', *Noûs* 1, reprinted in Loux (ed.) (1979) *The Possible and the Actual.* Ithaca, NY: Cornell University Press.
Dretske, F. (1977). 'Laws of Nature', *Philosophy of Science* 44.
Drewery, A. (2001). 'Dispositions and *Ceteris Paribus* Laws', *British Journal for the Philosophy of Science* 42: 723–733.
Ellis, B. and Lierse, C. (1994). 'Dispositional Essentialism', *Australasian Journal of Philosophy* 72.
Ellis, B. (2001). *Scientific Essentialism.* Cambridge: Cambridge University Press.
—— (2002). *The Philosophy of Nature.* Chesham: Acumen.
—— (2006). 'Universals, the Essential Problem and Categorical Properties', this volume.
Kripke, S. (1980). *Naming and Necessity.* Oxford: Blackwell.
Lange, M. (2002). *The Philosophy of Physics.* Oxford: Blackwell.
Lewis, D. (1970). 'How to Define Theoretical Terms', *Journal of Philosophy* 67.
—— (1973). *Counterfactuals.* Oxford: Blackwell.
—— (1986). *On the Plurality of Worlds.* Oxford: Blackwell.
—— (2002). 'Ramseyan Humility', unpublished typescript.
Martin, C. B. (1994). 'Dispositions and Conditionals', *Philosophical Quarterly* 44.
Mellor, D. H. (1974). 'In Defence of Dispositions', *Philosophical Review* 83.
—— (2000). 'The Semantics and Ontology of Dispositions', *Mind* 109: 757–80.
Molnar, G. (2003). *Powers: A Study in Metaphysics*, ed. S. Mumford. Oxford: Oxford University Press.
Mumford, S. (1998). *Dispositions.* Oxford: Oxford University Press.
—— (2004). *Laws in Nature.* London: Routledge.
Pargetter, R. J. and Prior, E. (1982). 'The Dispositional and the Categorical', *Pacific Philosophical Quarterly* 63.
Prior, E. (1985). *Dispositions.* Aberdeen: Aberdeen University Press.

Rovelli, C. (1997). 'Halfway Through the Woods: Contemporary Research in Space and Time', in *The Cosmos of Science: Essays of Exploration*, ed. J. Earman and J. Norton. Pittsburgh: University of Pittsburgh Press.

Shoemaker, S. (1984). 'Causality and Properties', in *Identity, Cause, and Mind*. Cambridge: Cambridge University Press: 206–33.

Smolin, L. (1991). 'Space and Time in the Quantum Universe', in *Conceptual Problems of Quantum Gravity*, ed. A. Ashtekar and J. Stachel. Boston: Birkhauser.

Swoyer, C. (1982). 'The Nature of Natural Laws', *Australasian Journal of Philosophy* 60.

Tooley, M. (1977). 'The Nature of Laws', *Canadian Journal of Philosophy* 7.

CHAPTER 6

UNIVERSALS, THE ESSENTIAL PROBLEM AND CATEGORICAL PROPERTIES

Brian Ellis

1. Universals

The ontology of my *Scientific Essentialism* (hereafter *SE*) is like E. J. Lowe's four category theory (Lowe 1998: ch. 9). But if Lowe's ontology is four category, then, by the same method of counting, mine is six. In Lowe's theory, there are two kinds of universals (substantive and non-substantive) ranging over two kinds of particulars (substances and modes). In mine, there are three kinds of universals (substantive, tropic and dynamic) ranging over three kinds of particulars (substances, tropes and events). Lowe's substantive and non-substantive universals are, as far as I can see, exactly the same as my substantive and tropic ones, and his modes are exactly the same as my tropes. Evidently, though, he does not believe that he needs to accommodate the possibilities of change in the same kind of way. In postulating the existence of dynamic universals, I assume that there are natural kinds of change that have particular changes as their instances. That there are natural kinds of changes seems to me to be a clear consequence of the postulate that there are causal powers in nature, and that these causal powers have specific instances. For, (a) the identity of a causal power can only depend on how it disposes its bearer to behave, and (b) causal powers of the same natural kinds must always be displayed in causal processes of the same natural kinds.

John Heil sees no valid role for universals of any kind in his ontology. He believes that it would be much better, and much less mystifying, to speak of natural similarity classes of tropes (or 'modes' as he prefers to call them). He admits that universals would be acceptable if he could make any sense of them. For they do at least seem to explain the existence of the similarity classes that properties represent. But he confesses that he finds universals unintelligible. So do I, if David Armstrong's theory of universals[1] is taken as our guide. But, I think Heil takes Armstrong's

---

[1] As developed in Armstrong (1989).

account of universals much too literally. His talk about universals being wholly present in each instance can do nothing but cause confusion. Universals do not have parts. So talk of their being wholly present is at best pleonastic. At worst, it suggests that universals are peculiar kinds of objects with an extraordinary property, viz. that of being wholly present in each of the objects that possess them. What he was getting at, I think, is just that universals are not to be confused with composite objects. We could, if we wished, speak of the composite object whose parts are all the red things in nature. But this would not be the universal, redness (if there were such a thing). It would just be a bearer of redness that includes all of the other bearers of redness as proper parts.

I compare universals with natural objects. Natural objects are to be distinguished from nominal objects, i.e. objects that are nominal fabrications. Brian Ellis, for example, is a natural object. It has its own distinctive history, spatiotemporal integrity, and continuity of properties. It is, in this sense, one natural bit of reality. Non-Brian Ellis, on the other hand, is a mere nominal object. It is created by the verbal trick of referential negation. There is no property, other than the fictitious property of not being Brian Ellis that is distinctive of it. The conjunctive object whose parts consist of Brian Ellis and John Heil is likewise not a natural object. If the world contains A and B as objects, it does not also contain the conjunctive object AB. Nor is the disjunctive object that consists of the thing that is either Brian Ellis or John Heil a natural object – for the same sort of reason. In general, there is no ontological principle that permits automatic recognition of negative, conjunctive or disjunctive natural objects. It is much the same with properties. There are natural properties and nominal properties. A natural property exists independently of our knowledge or understanding of it. It not a linguistic entity, and it is there in the world for us to discover. The grammatically permissible manoeuvres of predicate negation, conjunction and disjunction certainly generate new predicates. But they do not increase our knowledge of what there is. They only create the illusion of doing so. As I have argued at length in *SE*, the logical operators and connectives that apply to predicates ascribing natural properties to things do not automatically generate the names of new properties. That would be magical. Natural properties have to be discovered, and either named or described. There is no linguistic shortcut to such discovery.

If the things I call properties are natural divisions of the real world, just as the things I call natural objects are, then the same is true of all of the things in the other four ontological categories. They all exist and have their identities independently of how we choose to describe the world. Natural kinds of objects exist in this way, as chemists have known for at least two centuries. Natural kinds of events and processes involving such objects also exist, as every chemical equation attests. There literally are hundreds of thousands of such processes already known to us, and if we do not have names for all of them, we are certainly able to offer definite descriptions of them. As with the objectual and property universal divisions of reality, grammatical operations on the names or definite descriptions of things in these other categories do not yield new knowledge. There are no conjunctive or disjunctive natural kinds. There might occasionally be a pair of mutually exclusive and jointly exhaustive natural kinds in a given category. But, if so, this is something we should have to discover by the legitimate methods of science. The grammatical operation of negation cannot yield such knowledge.

For these formal reasons, I find it useful to think of natural kinds (whether of tropes, objects or events) as part of the furniture of the world. Consistently with what I have said so far, I suppose one could go along with John Heil's idea that natural kinds are just natural similarity classes of one kind or another. But there is, quite independently of the formal similarity that I have noted between kinds and objects, a powerful reason to develop a realistic ontology of natural kinds, viz. that the natural kinds all exist in hierarchies, and that this hierarchical structure of reality provides a good, and, as far as I know, the only satisfactory account of the hierarchical structure of natural laws (*SE*, Ch. 6).

2. The essential problem

Stephen Mumford is worried about my ontology for a very different reason. He accepts that there are natural properties and natural kinds of objects, all of which are universals of one kind or another. Natural properties are universals whose instances are modes (or 'tropes' in my terminology), and natural kinds of objects do, of course, have natural objects as their instances. But Mumford is not convinced that there is any need for my further postulate that natural kinds must have real essences, i.e., sets of intrinsic properties or structures in virtue of which things that belong to the natural kinds are things of the kinds they are. 'To be essential', he says, 'a property must be instantiated by every kind member, plus have some extra feature' (p. 51). But, what is this extra feature?

My answer now, as it was in *SE*, is simply *causal explanatory power*. The concept of intrinsicality used in *SE* is a causal one that reflects the common structure of causal explanations in science. In all such explanations, a distinction is made between what is due to the intrinsic properties or structures of things, and what is due to extrinsic forces acting upon them. The external forces are those that are due to the physical circumstances of a thing's existence. Therefore, the external component of any scientific causal explanation is always contingent. But the intrinsic properties and structures of things are the properties or structures that the things are supposed to have independently of their circumstances. And, it is not obvious that these too must be contingent.

Normally, our knowledge of the intrinsic properties or structures of things of various kinds derives from the predictive success or otherwise of the theoretical postulates we make concerning their constitutions. These postulates, if true, may well be necessarily true, since it may well be the case that, if the things in question did not have the constitutions that they are theoretically supposed to have, then they would not be things of the kinds they are. The properties or structures I call 'essential to things of a kind K' are just those that a rational scientific inquirer would ultimately have to make concerning the intrinsic properties and structures things of this kind, whatever the circumstances of its existence. It is true that some intrinsic properties or structures are acquired, and therefore contingent. The brittleness of a piece of metal, for example, may be changed by manipulation. So, no particular degree of brittleness can be an essential property of a metal. But scientific inquirers should have no difficulty in identifying which properties or structures are thought to be essential. The supposed chemical constitution of water, for example, is thought to be an essential property of water. A liquid sample that did not have this chemical constitution would not be considered to be water. It is also true that statements attributing essential properties to natural kinds are *a posteriori*, and therefore open to empirical refutation. Nevertheless, if they are true, then they are necessarily true – which is all that essentialism requires.

Mumford speculates that we could well accept that there are natural kinds of objects, without believing in essences. For the similarities of the members of such a kind would be adequately explained, he thinks, by their being instances of the same substantive universal. But this attributes far more explanatory power to universals than they can possibly provide. They are not templates that stamp out the objects that are their instances, as a biscuit cutter stamps out biscuit shapes. Rightly conceived, universals are just natural ways in which the most primitive particulars of the three basic categories of things are divided. Consequently, the fact that something is a member of a natural kind tells us very little about it, and does not explain why it is like the other things of its kind. The task of metaphysics is to explain the bases of these natural divisions, and the essentialist hypothesis is part of this project.

On inspection, it is clear that the ways in which reality is divided are not mutually independent, but have a natural hierarchical structure. The three kinds of universals already distinguished – substantive, tropic and dynamic – refer to the natural ways that primitive objects, tropes and events are classified. But not all universals are equally fundamental, because there are relationships of ontological dependence between them. The most fundamental are the most general, i.e., the category-wide universals that have all things in their respective categories as instances. The category-wide universals are the physical system, the physical property and the physical event. Every more specific universal is ontologically dependent on the genera of which it is a species. For nothing could be an instance of a specific universal without being an instance of every more general kind to which it necessarily belongs. Therefore every specific universal that is a member of any of the natural kinds hierarchies must at least have an essence that derives from its position in the hierarchy. For example, every sample of chlorine is necessarily a sample of a halogen, which is necessarily a chemical element, which is necessarily a substance with an atomic-molecular structure, which is necessarily a physical system.

However, the essences of the natural kinds do not derive simply from their positions in the natural kinds hierarchies. If our science is right, the essences are the postulated intrinsic causes of the manifest properties and behaviour of the substances in question. Or, if we are dealing with natural kinds of processes, then their essences are the intrinsic causal powers that are displayed in these processes. In either case, sameness of essence implies sameness of kind, and difference of essence implies difference of kind. Two samples of uranium, for example, may be chemically identical, and otherwise very difficult to tell apart. But one may be the highly dangerous U^{235} and the other the relatively innocuous U^{238}. Similarly, we may have two spectra that are hard, or even impossible, to tell apart. Nevertheless, the processes of which these spectra are displays may be very different from each other. For one might be a display of refractivity, while the other is a display produced by diffraction. What holds for these cases holds in general. For in every case, it is the essence, identified by its causal role, which defines the natural kind. It is plausible, therefore, to suggest that natural kinds without essences are ontologically suspect. But we must not be too hasty.

Biological kinds would appear to be natural kinds without essences. For, although they are like natural kinds in many ways, they do not have essences in quite the way that chemical substances do. Their similarities are due to the importance of their genetic constitutions in explaining their morphological characteristics. Their dissimilarities are due to the variance and evolution over time of their genetic constitutions. The existing species of animals and plants are therefore just clusters of morphologically similar organisms whose similarities are due to their genetically similar constitutions. Hence, our species concepts are generic cluster concepts. They are not, however, generic kinds that are categorically distinct from one another, as the generic chemical kinds are. The species 'elephant' has a number of subspecies, which are sub-clusters within the elephant cluster, that are distinct enough to be reliably distinguished morphologically, and sufficiently different genetically to be said to be different kinds of animals. However, if we broadened our vision to include all of the ancestors of the current elephants in the world, we should find, I think, that the morphological clusters, and the genetic clusters that explain them, would shift about as we go back in time, and eventually overlap. Therefore, neither the generic species, nor any subspecies, of elephant is a natural kind in the same sense as the generic and specific chemical kinds are. Chlorine, for example is a generic chemical kind, the species of which include the various isotopes of chlorine. But there is no species of chlorine existing now, or at any other time, that could possibly be a species of any element other than chlorine. Chlorine, the generic kind, has a fixed nature, and each species of chlorine has its own fixed nature.

Humean natural kinds are much more suspect ontologically. If substantive universals had only the members of Humean kinds as instances, then we should not think that substantive universals were a significant ontological category. An inkblot, a lake and a birthmark could, for example, all accidentally have the same shape, and be the only objects in the universe that happened to have this shape. But, given their diverse constitutions, there would be no reason to think that the similarity of these objects was due to anything other than a freak accident. Because of their distinctive similarity, I suppose, that they could be said to be members of a natural kind. But, if so, it would be a natural kind with a difference. For there are no intrinsic causal powers that could possibly explain the existence of this kind. Hence, if there were an essence of this kind, it could only be a nominal essence.[2]

Mumford also suggests that we could reasonably believe in causal powers, without being essentialists. But I find this suggestion rather hard to fathom. Firstly, the existence of causal powers clearly entails the existence of natural kinds of processes. In particular, it implies the existence of at least some of those kinds of processes that are the displays of these powers. Moreover, the powers in question are necessarily of the essence of these processes. A process of refraction, for example, must be due to the refractivity of some material. A mock-up case of refraction using concealed diffraction gratings would not be a process of refraction, however well it imitated the real thing. Secondly, the real essences of the substantive natural kinds are the intrinsic causal powers that members of these kinds must have if their manifest properties and overt behaviour are to be causally explained. So, one of the primary reasons for believing in causal powers is precisely that we must postulate them to explain what real essences do for the things that have them. If someone does not have this reason for believing in them, because they do not believe in the kinds of explanations that require things to have intrinsic causal powers, as most scientific explanations seem to do, then I think we are owed an account of scientific explanation that requires causal powers, but does not require that things must

---

[2] Remember that shape is not necessarily an intrinsic property on my account of intrinsicality. See my *Scientific Essentialism*, pp. 26–30.

belong to the natural kinds they do because of their causal powers.

3. Categorical properties

Alexander Bird raises the important issue of strong versus weak dispositional essentialism, and argues the case for the strong version of this doctrine. Weak dispositional essentialism is the thesis that some properties, including many of those that figure in the fundamental laws of nature, are essentially dispositional. This is the thesis defended by Caroline Lierse and me in our 1994 paper. The strong version is Sydney Shoemaker's (1980) claim that what makes a property the property it is, what determines its identity, is its potential for contributing to the causal powers of things that have it. The issue is important because acceptance of the strong version of dispositional essentialism would appear to be incompatible with the view that there are genuine categorical properties in nature, i.e., weak categoricalism.

Bird's case for the strong version of dispositional essentialism is presented in his section entitled 'Against Quidditism'. This section concludes:

> We do not want our metaphysics of properties to condemn us to necessary ignorance of them. And so we should reject quidditism. Since categoricalism entails quidditism (strong and weak), we should reject categoricalism too. The problems concerning identity and reference raised by quidditism are immediately resolved by adopting strong dispositional essentialism, the view that the identity of properties is fixed by their essential powers (p. 79).

Heil's case is likewise based on the unknowability of powerless categorical properties. But rather than opt for a world of naked powers, Heil makes the classical Lockean compromise. He thinks that the world is fundamentally one made up of 'powerful qualities' – a world that is neither one of naked powers, nor one that is purely qualitative.

To deal with this problem, I defend a compatibilist thesis. I say that a property can have a causal role without either being a causal power, or being ultimately reducible to causal powers. For even the most fundamental causal powers in nature have dimensions. They may be located or distributed in space and time, have magnitude, be one or many in number, be scalar, vector or tensor, alternate, propagate with the speed of light, radiate their effects uniformly, and so on. But these dimensions of the powers are not themselves causal powers. A location in space and time is not itself located or in space and time. Nor does having a magnitude have a magnitude. Nor is being one or many in number itself one or many in number. Yet these dimensions of the powers clearly do have causal roles. They not only signify the respects in which causal powers may be similar or different from one another, their detailed specification is required to define the laws of distribution, action and effect of the powers. These dimensions of the causal powers are the properties that I call categorical. They are real, and no less important in the overall scheme of things than the causal powers that have them essentially. In reality, they are second order properties – properties of properties. They are, indeed, amongst the essential properties of the causal powers.

Bird defines a categorical property:

> ... as [one that] does not confer of necessity any power or disposition. Its existence does not, essentially, require it to manifest itself in any distinctive fashion in response to an appropriate stimulus. To say that a property is categorical is to deny that it is essentially dispositional (p. 65).

The dimensions of the causal powers, which normally must be specified to define their essential natures, are plausibly categorical in this sense. For the dimensions of the causal powers are not properties that things could have independently of the powers. They simply would not exist if the powers did not exist. Nevertheless, most of the powers that do exist in the world could not exist without them. For a dimensionless power would have to be one that had no directed law of action, no law of combination with other powers, whether of the same or different kinds, and no law of action that refers to anything other than the events that are supposed to be causally connected. It would have to be a very simple kind of causal power – perhaps one that could be adequately analysed conditionally as 'If X were to happen, then Y would happen'. But most powers are not dimensionless like this. For we do not live in a dimensionless world, and how things act and interact with each other depends on how they are distributed and oriented, and what powers, capacities and propensities they all have. Consider gravity. There is a law of distribution of gravitational forces $f = -Gm_1 m_2/r^2$, a law of action of gravitational forces $f = ma$, and a vector law of addition of gravitational forces. Therefore, the causal powers of things cannot be specified zero-dimensionally. To describe the causal powers of things it is necessary to say what they would do to what in whatever circumstances.

The dimensions of the powers do not, of themselves, confer of necessity any powers or dispositions on things. Nevertheless, they will need to be specified if we are adequately to define what the powers and dispositions of things are. The spatiotemporal separation between two objects is a real objective property of those objects. But its existence does not essentially require them to behave in any particular way. Let them be connected by a piece of string (as in Newton's 'twin globes' thought experiment). Then let us cut the string. How the objects will then behave must depend on many things besides their spatiotemporal separation – on the shapes and mass distributions within the objects, on their respective masses, on whether they are charged or electrically neutral, and on whether the system is inertial or not. Of course, one can build all of these factors into one's description of the situation and declare that if the string is cut in these circumstances, then such and such must happen. But note that the factors that must be specified now include all of the causal powers that are operating. Spatiotemporal relations are therefore powerless without the causal powers to animate them, just as the causal powers would have to be dimensionless, as in a sort of Turing machine, if there were no spatiotemporal relations.

References

Armstrong, D. M. (1989). *Universals: An Opinionated Introduction*. Boulder, San Francisco, London: Westview Press.

Bird, A. (2006). 'Laws and Essences', this volume.

Ellis, B. D. (2001). *Scientific Essentialism*. Cambridge: Cambridge University Press.

Ellis, B. D. and Lierse, C. (1994). 'Dispositional Essentialism', *Australasian Journal of Philosophy* 72: 27–45.

Heil, J. (2006). 'Kinds and Essences', this volume.

Lowe, E. J. (1998). *The Possibility of Metaphysics: Substance, Identity, and Time*. Oxford: Clarendon Press.

Mumford, S. (2006). 'Kinds, Essences, Powers', this volume.

Shoemaker, S. (1980). 'Causality and Properties', in *Time and Cause*, ed. P. van Inwagen. Dordrecht: Reidel Publishing Co.: 109–35.

INDEX

Printed and bound by CPI Group (UK) Ltd, Croydon, CR0 4YY

13/04/2025

14656563-0001